The Dollar Compendium

A selection from

The Dollar Magazine

Compiled by R R Cumming

Published 2009
by
The Dollar Compendium
15 Harviestoun Road
Dollar
FK14 7HG

Printed in Great Britain by
Barr Printers Limited
Moray House, 4 Faraday Road, Southfield Estate, Glenrothes, Fife KY6 2RU

ISBN No. 978-0-9564396-0-4

Table of Contents

Introduction

Introduction

After my parents died we were clearing their house of the mountain of books they had accumulated over the years. Among a varied collection of novels, biographies and many other subjects I found a full collection of first editions of The Dollar Magazine from 1902 to 1910 and various other editions up to the 1950's. I was aware that the Dollar Museum has a full collection of these magazines and that they would not need another set so they were placed in a cardboard box to go out in the next trip to the skip.

I sat down beside this box at one point and idly picked one up and read an article. "That's quite interesting" I thought, and put the book back in the box. As it happened, the skip load was full and we left it there for the next week. The same thing happened the next weekend. I sat down with a cup of coffee and read one of Miss Christie's travelogues and imagined the difficulties of a single lady from a small village in Clackmannanshire travelling all that way in 1903.

By this time the cardboard box was beginning to receive some protection from me. I was moving it around the house to various corners so that it did not make its final journey, without letting on to the others who, by this time, were throwing out things without restraint. I had to come clean. Like a character from a Bateman cartoon I confessed and said I wanted to keep them.

It is worth remembering that the Dollar Magazine was first produced at the beginning of the twentieth century in a village of some 1500 inhabitants. No metropolis. The articles are well written, diverse in content, and, I have to warn those of a politically correct persuasion, contemporary. What an astonishing range of places they came from: Morocco, Korea, China, Brazil, even the Balearic Islands! Most were from Former Pupils telling of their work where they were and their impressions of the country. However, and poignantly, there are also letters from the front in the First World War, from young men who would never come back. The magazine regularly gave lists of those who had died.

I thought that there would be many people who would be interested in reading some of them so have compiled this collection. The choice was mine and they are completely at random. Dear reader, please remember that these were written for the time. They were for an ephemeral magazine and no one expected them to be read a century later so please make some allowances. It is an interesting piece of social history.

My thanks go to a number of people who helped me with the preparation of the book. In particular I would like to thank Janet Carolan for the biographies, to Jennifer Campbell for the illustrations and to Angus McLean and Peter Nelson for the jacket cover. I would also thank Morna Small without whose help the book would never have been completed and Catherine Shaw and Richard Dunning for their help with the compilation.

R.R.Cumming   September 2009

Chapter One

Adventure

Notes from the Burmah Oilfields

By W J Drysdale

Dollar Magazine Vol. VIII No. 30 – June 1909

"There was a bit of a row at Bwetchie two days before I left. The Burmans had a big festival for about a week, and the last night of it I was down at the river-bank when I heard a fight going on in the village. It turned out to be between Burma Oil Company's Indian coolies and Burmans. Needless to say, I did not wait to see who was at fault, but fixed on the first coolie I met. I managed to get the fight stopped, but not before one Indian was laid out with a club. I worked at him for an hour or so, but could not get him back to consciousness, so he died. He had got a smash on the back of the head. I don't think it takes much to kill a coolie.

"I saw a well 'flowing' yesterday (you could call it 'spouting'). The oil was going up into the air 30 to 40 feet – beautiful, clean, reddish oil. Oh, for a well like that in the back garden. Derricks 70 to 80 feet high everywhere, steam-engines and boilers galore. The gas pressure in the wells is enormous, forcing the oil up so high as it does. Of course they don't let it spout all the time. They shut it in as soon as they can get the boring tools out of the well, which is about 2,300 feet deep. The native wells are holes 4 feet square, dug by hand to a depth of 200 or 300 feet. The oil filters in to a depth of a few feet, then two or three men or women take it out with a kerosene can attached to a rope. They now use a modified diver's helmet and air-pump to dig these wells, the digger working by reflected light sent down by a mirror at the surface, as the gas precludes lamplight below. The diver's apparatus came into use only six or seven years ago.

"An old Burman pearl-diver was travelling on a Flotilla steamer with his machine on his way to the ruby mines, and happening to meet two Burmese well-owners, they began talking, and mentioned that they had to have a relay of men to dig their wells, as one could stay down only a few minutes, so they persuaded him to get off and go with them to the wells. They got a Burman to don the diving dress, screwed-down helmet, and lead-soled shoes; they blew him up and lowered him down the four-foot hole. The natives turned out in hundreds to view this wonderful thing. In a minute the diver signalled to be pulled up. When the helmet was off they asked him why he did not dig, did he not get air? Oh, yes, the air was all right, but he was blown up so big that he could not bend in the four-foot hole, far less dig. When the pearl-diver knew it was a case of working in two feet or so of liquid, he got a tin helmet made, and discarded the dress and lead shoes, and this is still the way the natives dig their wells."

The Death of a Man-eater

Extract of Letter from Sylhet, Assam

By A W Strachan

Dollar Magazine Vol. VI No. 22 – June 1907

"I am sending you a photo of one of the tigers that has been killing such a lot of cows round here lately. I had been watching the brute's tracks for weeks, and finding out his regular beats we then decided to try and tempt him with a goat. The moon was nearly full and we got a 'mâchan' made in a tree at one end of the coolies' rice fields, and decided to tie up the goat there and see what would happen, though I don't think either of us imagined for a moment that we would see the tiger. However, we could but try and it was better to sacrifice a goat than for the coolies to lose all their cows; so we got a fat one that was destined to be turned into 'mutton' in any case, and tied him up about twenty yards away from the 'mâchan'.

"We went out soon after dark and made ourselves as comfortable as possible in a very small space and waited. You can have no idea how interesting it is sitting up like that at night, as you see things and hear sounds that you would seldom see or hear in the daytime. Perhaps you can understand that when you are sitting up for a tiger every little sound is exaggerated and you can imagine a pair of gleaming eyes looking at you out of every dark patch in the jungle.

"To the initiated the 'gleaming eyes' are nothing more formidable than fire-flies, and the rustling of leaves is generally made by a lizard or a rat, though occasionally a sounder of pig or a deer goes crashing past with noise enough to make a timid person imagine that all the tigers in creation are coming for him.

"It was a glorious night, almost light enough to read, so there was not much difficulty in seeing if anything did come. At about ten o'clock a barking deer 'barked' a long way off, a sure sign that it had been startled by something. This made us 'sit up' a bit, but another hour passed without anything happening, then a hog deer gave a squeak, and crashed away through the jungle about half a mile away. This made us pretty sure that something was on the prowl, and we began to get excited. However, still another hour passed and nothing came, and we were beginning to get tired of it, when all of a sudden a long, lithe beast jumped from behind a bush about fifty yards away, and with a few easy bounds was on to the wretched goat, which was sent to 'kingdom come', I suppose, before it had time to realise what was happening. R. and I fired together, but A. had been half asleep and did not grasp the situation till the tiger was making tracks back to the jungle. I was certain my bullet had struck the beast and R. was pretty sure his had, and we were very much astonished to see the brute go off apparently untouched.

"We got down from the mâchan and went cautiously to the end of the jungle where the tiger had disappeared, and, as we could hear it struggling a short way in, we came to the conclusion that it was wounded, probably badly.

"It would have been absolute folly to have followed it up then as it was pitch dark under the trees, so we went back to R.'s bungalow to wait for daylight, sleep being out of the question. The moment it was light enough to see we went back with half a dozen coolies, and found blood

4

tracks where we had seen the tiger disappear into the jungle. These we followed up, having to cut our way through for about a hundred yards, when we heard the brute growl some way ahead. We went very cautiously after that, you may be sure, and I being first was keeping my eyes very much about me. All of a sudden an *unwounded* tiger seemed to rise out of the ground about ten yards from me, and, before I had time to put my gun to my shoulder he turned round and bounded into the jungle and disappeared. He was evidently waiting for us, but came to the conclusion that discretion was the better part of valour against such odds, luckily for me, as I wouldn't have had time to get out of his way if he had charged. Neither of the others saw him as they were behind.

"After that I went to cut off the wounded one which was gradually working round a small hill. I went round the other side and got within three yards of it before I knew. Luckily its back was turned to me and I gave it a shot in the back of the head. Even then it had strength enough left to give a very intimidating roar, but it was its last.

"It proved to be a very old tigress with a broken canine tooth, which was probably the reason she had taken to 'cattle lifting'. When they get old, tigers have scarcely sufficient energy to pull down deer and it is then that they take to man-eating as they find him a very easy prey. It was well her career ended when it did as most probably she would have become a man-eater before very long."

About the author: He was the son of Dr Strachan Jnr and lost an arm and a leg in India after an attack by a tiger. He returned to Dollar and wrote a book *"Mauled by a Tiger"*. Latterly he ran Brookside boarding house.

Mission Life in Morocco

"Among the Arabs"

By Johan W Learmond

Dollar Magazine Vol. VI No. 22 – June 1907

In Morocco as elsewhere there are different classes in the community. Our mission being to either the palace or the hut, wherever we might be called, we were thus brought into touch with all classes. I have thought it might be of interest to the readers of the *Dollar Magazine* to hear something of the life and customs of the Bedouin Arabs. Direct descendants of Ishmael they claim to be, and their whole appearance points to the truth of him being their forefather. Their mode of life and customs also take one back to the old world when Hagar was sent forth from the tent of Abraham with her son Ishmael. In certain districts we have those Arabs dwelling in tents or hive-shaped huts. Among the tent-dwellers we have been called to minister, so I give our experience of one such journey and visit as it remains in my memory to-day.

One morning in our dispensary work there came two men with a story of a poor suffering woman lying very ill out in the country. Would we not satisfy her desire and go to see her, even although we might not be able to help her much? On consideration we decided to return with them the following day. Preparation had to be made as it meant a day's journey. We knew not to depend too much on Moorish calculation of time. Before daybreak we (our escort and two Arab friends) started off. We had luckily good-going mules, but our Arab friends had one donkey between them, and took turns alternately of riding. It was intensely amusing to hear the language addressed to that poor donkey – "May your father be burned for having such a lazy offspring," or "No, he is not worth burning, he must have been a pig," the lowest of all animals in the eyes of a Moor. But the poor donkey heeded not the high-flown language levelled at him, and waited his own time of quietly paying his master back. How he could double up his legs and lie down, which meant respite from a heavy load for a short time at least. As we passed along the highway we met camel-drivers or travellers, with whom "where were we going" was the question generally asked.

The sun was now up in full strength, we were out on an open plain, not a blade of grass nor tree to be seen; it was late summer, all the crops had been gathered in, and everything was dried up. Water was also scarce, so when there appeared to our view away in the distance a lovely lake bordered with waving palm-trees, now, we thought, that's the place where we can rest a little in the share and get cool. But, alas, we never seemed to get nearer the cool stream, and all at once the picture disappeared; it was only a mirage which appears to travellers on the plains. We were still miles off from the nearest well, and before we reached it we had dismounted and had lunch. It was too hot to remain on the bare hillside so we pushed on to the place for watering our animals.

Here we had a typical Eastern scene. All the flocks from the surrounding farms were gathered, waiting for the water to be drawn up, for "the well was deep," and it meant time and hard work to get a *pitcher* filled. Our escort was known to some of the men in charge of the flocks, and they kindly let us have our turn drawing the water so that we might get on quickly. I seemed to be a bit of a novelty to them: "Is it a man or a woman?" In travelling we veil up our eyes, so our sex and mode of riding are always a puzzle to those country people. "You are only an hour from your destination," we were informed as we left. That hour lengthened into two and a half hours, so our surmise was correct – the journey of six hours turned out to be one of nine and a half hours.

Just before sunset we arrived at the Arab village. We had a stiff ride up to it, as the tents were right up on a hillside. We had been observed coming in the distance, and quite a number of men, women, and children met us by the wayside and bade us welcome. Kindness and hospitality to strangers is the outstanding characteristic among all classes in Morocco, at least we have always found it so, even although

7

we were of the hated Nasara. We knew we were among a people who, if the fanatical spirit were aroused, would not hesitate to slay and kill; but we were under their protection and felt perfectly safe, as those who had brought us would see that nothing would be done to molest us. Agriculture is the only means of livelihood with the Arabs, so in this village of tents each seemed to have a piece of ground cultivated. Unfortunately they are all heavily taxed by Government, and it matters not whether the year be good or bad, those taxes must be paid. One is not surprised at the desperate means sometimes used to get hold of money to pay up.

The women and children crowded round, and we had to answer the usual questions as to our country, parentage, married or single, &c. &c. We thought the women looked very picturesque, dressed in a dark-blue veil, draped and fastened at the shoulders with silver pins, and with ornaments of beads around their necks and also in their hair. Nearly all had their faces tattooed on the forehead, chin, and right down to the chest. Their carriage would be the envy of many of our English friends. They walk very gracefully; this having been acquired by the carrying of the water-pots on their heads. It never ceased to be a wonder to me how those Arab women could balance a water-pot, by no means small, on top of their head, and yet walk with such perfect ease and grace.

How primitive was the interior of the Arab home where we found our patient! A dark-coloured tent, one side being used for cooking, &c, the other side for sleeping. The utensils and furnishings could all be loaded on a donkey's back; and here, lying or rather sitting on a piece of matting, was the poor woman we had come to see and help if possible. We were too late; she was fast nearing the end, but she had wanted so much to see us, that her friends had the satisfaction of knowing they had done their best to give her this last desire.

The husband was very kind, indeed all the people were, and tried in their own way to make us feel at home. Food was brought, the national guest dish, kus-kus. A new hut had been got ready for our use, and we thought it looked all right. However, in this case appearances proved deceitful. We had rather a lively time of it with unmentionable live stock. After vainly trying to get to sleep, the discomfort got unbearable, so we drew our mattress to the outside of the hut. It was a close summer night, and all the village seemed to be sleeping in the open air. Just in front of our abode mules and donkeys were tethered; a little farther off were a number of cows, sheep, and goats. The green-looking bundles huddled up here and there were our native friends fast asleep. The occasional barking of dogs, the bleating of sheep, the crowing of a cock, were the only sounds that broke the stillness.

Our host was the first astir, and soon, just as the day began to break, the Arab village was all alive; the flocks driven out to pasture and the cows milked; and there was the grinding of the hand mill where the wheat was being ground to make hot cakes for our breakfast.

Once more we visited our poor friend, who seemed to be brighter, and thanked us warmly for coming to see her. Only a poor, suffering Arab woman, and yet with a heart to respond to kindness shown. We felt we had gained and been taught a lesson, as we left that Arab village on the hillside, that it was good to go at the call of duty, though it be to the highways or byways of Morocco.

Our animals seemed to know we were on the homeward journey, as we got into town in the early afternoon, having only taken eight hours to return. Quite long enough to be in the saddle, with only a short break of half an hour. But one gets accustomed to this mode of travelling in Morocco.

Mission Life in Morocco

"A Visit to a Governor's Harem"

By Johan W Learmond

Dollar Magazine Vol. VI No. 21 – March 1907

In Morocco the ladies of high officials are kept very secluded, and as it was our mission to try and get at them, we were glad to accept the invitation from the Governor to dine with him upon a certain day. We had only been a few weeks in the city (Marakesh), and knew very little of the language or customs of the people; but as the opportunity could not be allowed to pass, we hoped it would be our good fortune to get through the ordeal without any serious blunder.

The appointed day arrived, and early in the afternoon a slave came to escort us to the Governor's house, to which, as it was some distance, we had to ride. It was a bit of a novelty going out to dinner dressed in a riding habit. We knew, however, that the invitation was given to satisfy the curiosity of the harem ladies, who had heard about the arrival of the Christians. As we were the first they had seen, there was great excitement over our coming, and for the occasion they had put on their gayest and best robes and jewels.

On our arrival at the door some of the guard took charge of our animals, the huge door of entrance was unlocked by a porter, we passed in, and the door was locked. We felt as if we were inside a prison, and truly a Moorish harem is a prison. From an inner courtyard we were met by two stalwart ebony black slaves, who said in Arabic, "Our lord will be with you in a few minutes." Chairs were brought, and we waited for the coming of the Governor. The minutes seemed long, but Moors are never in a hurry, nor think anything of the passing of time, or keeping one waiting; however, at last his lordship appeared and received us very graciously. He had been in England with a Moorish Embassy, so could speak a little English, but he understood better what was said.

After salutations had been exchanged we were conducted by our host to the ladies' quarter; we passed through several courts, and then up a broad winding stair. The staircase was very beautifully inlaid with Mosaic work. When we reached the top corridor we were met by a number of eunuchs and female slaves, all gaily dressed in light colours. The reception or dining room was just adjoining. As we entered the door we felt dazzled with the bright colours, the decoration of the room being distinctly Oriental, with rich coloured carpets. The gaily dressed ladies (between thirty and forty of them) were seated on divans ranged around the room.

Our introduction to this company of ladies was rather funny, our host thus expressing himself as we entered the room, "Here they are." After that we sat down on the chairs that had been brought in for our special benefit. In a short time tea was made by two of the ladies (green tea highly flavoured with mint, &c., and very sweet). The glasses used are small, otherwise, to a beginner; it is a bit of an ordeal to drink Moorish made tea. The tea and cakes were served by little slave girls. Then, as we had time to look at our new Moorish friends, we could see that they wanted us to come nearer to them. An elderly lady, who was afterwards found to be the Governor's mother, invited me to sit beside her. She had such a kind face, and we managed to become quite good friends by signs and the few sentences of Arabic I had got hold of. Then she got up, and one by one a dozen blind Jewish musicians were led in; one was guided to the piano, and seemed to be the leader of the company, the others all got squatted around him, and the orchestra began. We thought they played well. While the music was going on we were asked by our host to be seated at a table. Moors do not sit at a table or use knives, forks, or spoons, or plates, but the Governor had these for special occasions, and we were to be entertained *à l'Anglaise*, although Moorish in style. None of the ladies joined us at the table, the Governor superintending the bringing in of the different dishes. As each was placed before us he always used the expression, *Kul* (eat, and you are welcome"). Native cookery was still new to us, so we did poor justice to the ample and rich fare provided. Our lady friends had the dishes passed on to them where they all remained seated on the divans, waited upon by the little slave girls. They seemed to enjoy the novelty of seeing us sit at a table, using knives and forks; to us it was as great a novelty to see them in companies of half a dozen eating out of one dish and calmly licking their fingers after eating. Water was brought later for them to wash their hands. Many of them were richly dressed in silk and satin, with lovely strings of pearls and gold ornaments that must have cost a small fortune.

So fickle and uncertain are government positions in Morocco that to-day many of those ladies are almost beggars. The Governor having fallen into disgrace, his estates and nearly all he possessed taken from him, the best looking of his household taken into the palace, the others being sold as slaves; and so far as we know, he being either a prisoner or dead.

We finished dinner, then coffee and cakes were handed round, and after that dancing women were brought in. To us this part of the entertainment was not pleasant. The movements were not at all graceful, becoming faster and faster until the dancers sank down exhausted; a peculiar ringing cry they use sounded in our ears very weird; one felt in a land whose ways and customs were strangely different from those of our own country.

In the intervals of our entertainment we tried to make friends with some of the other ladies, but they were very shy. The Governor's chief wife (he had three others) was a very beautiful woman. She had two very pretty children, who while we were there were brought for us to see, but seemed so much afraid that they were soon taken away. Possibly they had been frightened by their nurses telling them we would take out their eyes to make medicine, or cut off their ears.

During all this time the Governor was the only gentleman present. The eunuchs and slaves are supposed to be a bodyguard; then the Jewish musicians were all blind, otherwise they would not have been allowed into the harem.

We thanked our host for his kind entertainment, when he gave us into charge of the guards, a dozen armed men, who escorted us safely through the dark crowded streets to our place of abode.

It was a new experience having an armed guard, and we were glad it was not to be an everyday one. The first dinner party in Morocco was not so trying as we had thought it would be.

In the Drakenberg Mountains
Fishing Trip to the Bushman's River

By Rev. J L Findlay, *Chaplain to the Forces*

Dollar Magazine Vol. X No. 37 – March 1911

We were a party of four. One was a lady, and one a parson. Can any sporting trip be successful without one or the other? Here we had both – best of auguries for a pleasant trip; and it was one of the pleasantest! We were all soldiers from Roberts' Heights – well – yes! I suppose the parson must be considered a soldier; is his name not in the Army List? and that too with crossed daggers in front. But the lady – well – no! Her name is not in the Army List, but does that really matter much – aren't there thousands of them in the army with never a name in the List?

Anyway we were from Roberts' Heights, Pretoria, and were bound for the upper reaches of the Bushman's River. Our object was fishing – fly-fishing for trout. Nothing but fly, and none but pounders and over, is an unwritten law on that fine stream. Escourt is the nearest railway station, and the train arrives there at 1 a.m. Out you stumble, wretched and cold; your rugs, fishing rods, landing nets, mosquito nets, luncheon basket and two kettles are soon bundled out after you. These are your light luggage – a bullock waggon laden with tents, tables, chairs, &c. – your heavy baggage lies out on the veldt, about a mile away, awaiting for you. The driver has strict orders to inspan at dawn. Oh, this start at daylight, so fearful, so uncomfortable, yet so necessary; it is one sovereign remedy against all difficulties connected with ox transport. It is a golden rule to get as much ground behind you as you possibly can before the sun gets hot. That is the reason why we repeated to ourselves over and over again in the train – "we must start at daybreak."

Oh gentle reader, if ever contemplating this trip you arrive at Escourt, and you can't roll yourself into a ball and crouch in a corner of the waiting-room from 1 a.m. till 5.30, then don't try – give it up – jump into the town 'bus and go comfortably to bed in the hotel; you can still fish the Bushman's River, and below the town drift you may even catch trout, but you will always be safe for a comfortable dinner and a game of billiards every evening. Make up your mind now while you are on the cold, bleak platform. If you can do without a wash and shave, and without shouting for a servant to bring you this or that, and if you are prepared to do manual labour on an empty stomach, then you belong to our guild, so come along with us, put your knees up to your chin, and go crouch in yonder corner, for at the first streak of daylight we are off, off to the mountains, where there is no billiards or smoking-room, no bar or lounge – the wet clothes you put off at night you put on next morning, just the same, only a little less wet.

It is not a usual thing to see white men carrying loads in Natal - that is black man's work – however, coolies or natives take some waking, and all that means time, so it is by necessity and not by choice that each of us could be seen humping his weary load at 5.30 towards the waggon, which, because of the cattle fever has to keep a mile away from the town. At last it is finished, every load is on board except the two kettles – these are in the lady's charge: from one she produces hard boiled eggs, and from the other hot steaming cocoa. We sit on the waggon, our legs dangling over the side, a cup of cocoa in one hand, an egg in the other, and our minds at ease. Jim, the driver, shoulders his long bamboo whip, casts his eye slowly round for a solemn last look, then with powerful lungs addresses "Appleman," "Snowball," "Waterman," "Paraffin," "Diamond," and each and every ox by its own peculiar name, and with a crack of his whip we are off up the hill, where you can see the last tiny star just fading away into the bluish grey of the far far beyond. Such a fine start had put everyone, both man and beast, in the best of moods, and when we outspanned at eleven o'clock we had covered three-quarters of that day's trek. We now had plenty of time for a wash, a shave, a change of clothes, and a comfortable breakfast. At two o'clock we are away again, and at five we arrived at the store, twenty-eight miles from our starting point, uphill all the way, the bullocks in the best of tempers, and looking forward to two hours' grazing before being put in their kraal for the night.

No person goes this trip, or any other trip in this direction up the Drakenbergs, but stays the night at the store at Tabenthlope. It is a fine example of what a store ought to be, and belongs to two of the best of fellows.

Tabenthlope means in the Zulu language "the Mountain with the White Cap." It is a huge mountain, comparatively small in area, but rises sheer some 3,000 feet from the very door of the store. Should the heavens contain any clouds, sooner or later during the day the mountain will push its nose into them. It is a fine sight to see a cloud slowly and majestically strike against this giant and slowly comb its course over his rough face, leaving streaks of white whiskers behind – hence the name, the mountain with the white cap. Well, we are at the store and are received by our hosts, for hosts they are – not a penny piece will they think of receiving for their hospitality, and it never occurs to you to suggest it. You are their guests. If you are members of the British Association, surveyors, policemen, missionaries, or any other person passing along, you are welcome.

"Come in and have some tea, we don't dine till eight." "Yes, your kit will be taken to your rooms." "You will have a fresh span of oxen to-morrow, so don't worry about that now, you will have plenty of time in the morning." "Ah, Colonel, back again, and our good friend, the Parson." "Well, the Missionary has gone further up the Berg, you will pass him to-morrow." "Ah yes, Colonel, this is Mrs ———. Pleased to meet you, hope you will like living under canvas." "Yes, Colonel, there has been a lot of rain up the Berg, you ought to catch some big ones this trip. By the way, Colonel, I can get none of our friends to believe that that big trout of yours, you caught last time, did really weight five pounds." "I want you, Mrs ———, to look at my strawberries after tea, they are literally in tons, lying rotting on the ground." "Next time you come, Parson, you must bring your choir boys and let them run wild." "Well, come in to tea."

That's the way you are received by the two storekeepers. A very learned man on a scientific exploration, a few years ago, received great help at their hands, he recorded their names in one of the scientific journals, so why should I keep silence? They are Messrs Couch and de Bathe. Both have been there for many years. They know the Zulu language as well as white men can know it. I know fewer hours more instructive than those spent in listening to the wonderful tales they can relate about the history of the African natives in general, and that of the Zulus in particular. They will tell you in detail about the extraordinary exploits of the Bushmen in the early days – how they used to come down from the mountains, hiding themselves in bushes during the day, and, only travelling by night, raid the horses and cattle of both the white and black man alike – how the Zulu and white combined forces in the late sixties and pursued them right up the Berg, driving them into the innermost caves of the very topmost ridges – how two whites were killed, and many blacks – how the Zulus returned with the women and children as war prisoners, and how, suddenly, one night many months afterwards, every Bushman prisoner, woman or child, suddenly vanished, and no one to this day knows how or where – how the feuds went on and on till at last the breechloader banished for ever every trace of the Bushman with his little bow and poisoned arrow, his implements of stone and wood. How, even to-day scientists come for guides to help and search the caves to try and find some real live Bushman, and can only find skeletons and broken water-pots. Thus, for hours, we listen as Mr Couch tells us the above and much more, then gives us his opinion upon the great racial question as it affects the Colonial.

"I dare say, Colonel," he goes on, "you will think us very ignorant up here, but we only get the weekly papers, and I should like so much to know about some of your problems. Now there is the education question, I feel sure it must be very important."

"Oh yes, oh yes," says the Colonel. "Now, Parson, you remember our discussion in the train, can't you go ahead? It's just five minutes to twelve, so be brief, old man; 'brevity is the soul of wit,' you know."

The Parson thus began: "Well, you see, my dear Couch, it's quite simple, it's a question of education – knowledge – wisdom, you know, and of course there is the religious side, too, you see. The bishops – yes, the Roman bishops as well, and the heads of the Dissenting bodies, all men of wisdom – all agree to meet together so that the children can have the benefit of their wis–––"

"Oh, dear, is that twelve striking?"

"What, would you credit it? The Colonel is fast asleep."

"Well, it must be bed. I will finish about the education question to-morrow."

Messrs Couch and de Bathe together: "Thank you, thank you, most interesting, most interesting."

The Colonel, very drowsily, "What, only weighs 2½ lbs? Well, I could have sworn––– Oh, pardon me, have I been asleep? Yes, I must have been nodding. Well, we've had a long journey. Well, good-night, good-night." And off we go to our rooms.

Next day our waggon is very heavily laden, for we take with us a fortnight's supply of stores of all kinds, including firewood.

Our friends have procured a native cook for us, and have arranged with a local runner to bring us our mail every second day, so, though now we will see no white faces but our own for fourteen days, we will still be in touch with civilisation. We have only nine miles to go, but one mile of that is along a road scratched out of the side of a precipitous hill. Crags, loose and ugly, tower above you on your left, and a nasty, shingly slope extends for a full thousand feet below on your right. It is a road full of possibilities. It is possible for the waggon to side-slip and tumble headlong down the ravine; that has happened several times. Once a canny Scot got so frightened with the narrow shaves his waggon was having that he outspanned and determined to wait for a day or more till the rain ceased and the road dried. The rain never ceased; it did the opposite – it came down in bucketfuls. A pool of water gathered round the base of the waggon wheels; soon it made a channel and began to pour over the edge of the road, and finally the whole road slipped clean away, taking the waggon with it, down to the bottom of the hill, and eventually dropping it a clean forty feet on to a big flat rock in the middle of the stream. It is in incidents like this that you detect the difference between the Englishman and Scotchman. You will, all over Africa, come across derelict waggons. They are all English. A Scotchman will spend days salving the very last piece of matchwood, and this Scotchman did the same in this case, but the big solid iron axle was too much for him, and there it lies on the flat rock to this day, for all the world like a big black snake basking in the sun, and it silently tells its tale. That happened long ago. They have now planted bushes on the dangerous side of the road, and their roots have bound the soil and stones together.

The gorge is soon passed, and now we are in quite a different country to anything we have yet seen. After passing many streams and crossing and recrossing the Bushman's River several times, we arrive at our camping ground. The natives have seen us long before this, and many willing hands are ready to help us pitch our tents and build a rough kitchen of turf and flat stones.

We have a late lunch, then each goes his own way, each is absent from tea, and each returns at dusk with half-a-dozen pounders for his first day's bag.

There is no spoiling that river, you can fish far apart or close to each other, it is always the same; you will get your pounders as regularly as night succeeds the day; you may take hours to locate them, for sometimes they are in the shallows or under the banks or in midstream, or they will only take big flies, or small flies, or a certain fly; you will find that out or your pal will whisper you the secret, and then you will, for anything from half-an-hour to two hours, have a glorious time, your piccaninny (small native boy) will open his mouth wider and wider as pounder after pounder he scoops into the landing net. After all that is just what makes the Bushman's River so fascinating; it is never the same and yet it is always the same. Never two days consecutively do the same tactics entice the pounders, yet before the day is finished you have always solved the problem; sooner or later you are almost always certain to have found out the one thing needful to put the pounders and yourself on terms of close acquaintance, and the whole thing may happen quite suddenly as if by magic.

How often have we compared notes at night and found the same changing conditions prevailed almost to minute detail with each of us, though we were fishing many miles apart.

Fourteen days seem too long to be always fishing, yet each of us fished every day except Sundays, and each of us had some fresh experience every day. I verily believe you could spend a whole season fishing every day on that river and learn something new each day. No part of the river seems to be better than another, and no pool seems to be the best. I have sometimes gone from pool to pool, creeping behind rocks and bushes with the idea of getting a three or a five-pounder, and I have found more than once that the lady of our party, blundering up with no such high hopes, has hooked and landed from the self-same pools three-pounders, and, as often as not, she has had the sun behind her. There are no grumblings, no rivalries, no jealousies on that river, for there is room for all. Only once did I feel anything approaching the miserable, and turned out to be the wretchedness of anticipation. I had been up the glen and it had begun to rain in torrents; very stupidly I took a short cut back to the tents, only to find the stream so high that I had to retrace my steps for miles up the glen again before I could cross, and then trudge back once more to the tents. As I approached I saw no sign of life, the kitchen was flooded, and the coolie cook, with his long lank hair looking like a drowned rat, sat shivering on the top of the stove and was speechless. I stumbled towards the mess tent with the object of having some Irish neat.

"Hullo, is that you?" came a cheery voice from within. "Crawl in under the flies, here's a mug of cocoa for you."

"Cocoa," I cried, "the very thing I have set my heart on. No, no I won't have any whisky, thank you; this cocoa is the best of drinks at present; but, I say, how did you boil the water?"

"Ah, the others asked me that also. I have a small spirit stove."

Yes! And what is more she had other things of which we were ignorant. That night, though it never ceased pouring, we had a fine supper all the same; there was camp pie, there was tongue, there was pickled trout and coffee afterwards, and all that we owed to the forethought of the one lady in our party.

I am now many thousand miles away, but I can still look back and see our four tiny tents nestling under the Giant's Castle, the highest and the grandest of all the peaks in the Drakenberg. I can still hear the river tearing its way, Spey-like, past our very doors; I can see the soft pool with its sandy bottom and the flat smooth rock above, where, with a hop, leap, and a bound from my tent, I used to stand morning after morning, hesitating and half funking, till with a "one, two, three," and closed eyes, I took a regular school-boy dive.

Now, gentle reader, if ever you have the opportunity, make your way to the Bushman's River, then, whether you be a fisherman or not a fisherman, you can experience in real life the meaning of that toast – the best of toasts, the fisherman's toast – "a tight line."

Captain Charles Williamson
1757 - 1808

By Rev. Robert Paul, F.S.A. Scot

Edited from the Dollar Magazine
Vol. VI No. 22 – June 1907

Alexander Williamson was born in Dumfries in 1724 and became secretary to the second Earl of Hopetoun. He became quite wealthy through his association with the Earl and the silver and lead mines of South Lanarkshire. In 1750 he and his wife Christian came to live in the Mains House in Dollar which stood until the present Dollar Academy dining hall and swimming pool was built in 1964. They were "native and kindly tenants" which meant that they held tenancy through succession by family and could not be evicted by

Photo by Mr R. K. Holmes.

WILLIAMSON'S MANOR HOUSE, DOLLAR.

the feu holder. When feudalism passed away they became practically the owners of the property.

Alexander and his wife Christian had three sons, Charles, John Hope and David. The career of the eldest, Charles Williamson, was the most remarkable and romantic. He was born in Edinburgh on 12th July 1757 and in 1775, at the age of 18, became an ensign by purchase in the 25th Regiment of Foot, then known as "The Edinburgh Regiment" afterwards as "The King's Own Borderers".

In 1777 he was promoted to the rank of Lieutenant, and four years later to that of Captain. At this time the American War of Independence was at its height, and France and Spain were in league with the colonies against the British. The 25th Regiment was sent to America, and in 1778 Charles Williamson was sent to join his regiment. The vessel, however, in which he sailed, was captured off Massachusetts by a French privateer and he was severely wounded during the battle. He was taken prisoner and sent to Boston where, as a prisoner on parole, he was billeted at the house of a family called Newell.

Charles spent three years with the Newell family where he was nursed through a long illness by the daughter of the house, Abigail. Abigail and Charles fell in love and when in an exchange of prisoners was made in 1781, Charles became a free man and proposed to Abigail. They were married in New London, Connecticut in 1784.

Abigail and Charles came back to the Mains House in Dollar, Charles having retired from the army on half pay. He travelled widely over the next few years, visiting Hungary, Turkey and Germany. In 1787 he moved from Dollar to Balgray in Dumfriesshire.

About this time a party of capitalists bought a tract of land from the United States Authorities consisting of over 2 million acres of land or 3500 square miles called the Genesee Tract. For this they paid a sum of £75,000, a very large sum of money in those days. The territory extended from the border of Pennsylvania on the south to Lake Ontario on the north, and from Seneca Lake on the east to the Genesee River on the west. A vast tract of wilderness, it was the undiscovered abode of the panther and the wolf. The broad valleys were covered with dense trackless forests unbroken in every direction. The hilltops were covered in white pines, dark and sombre, adding at least a hundred feet to their apparent height. The only human beings who had penetrated the forests had been native Indians. Today the area is in up-state New York and its two largest cities are Rochester on Lake Ontario and Buffalo on Lake Erie.

Charles was given the job of factor because the investors thought that his knowledge, energy and experience made him eminently suitable to develop its nascent resources, and to sell off blocks or allotments. He took on the job and with a band of courageous Scotsmen set off for the New World. He landed with his family in Norfolk Virginia in 1791 and set up in Philadelphia. The first thing he had to do was to appear before the Supreme Court of the new commonwealth of Pennsylvania and legally qualify himself to hold and dispose of land by taking the oath of allegiance. At this time it was impossible for aliens to hold land in the State of New York and it is quite remarkable that the party of investors put such trust in Captain Williamson since he would effectively be the sole owner of the area.

The lands were very far from the centres of civilisation in the New World and the difficulty of reaching them was increased by the entire absence of roads of any kind, while the navigation of the rivers, many of them large and broad, was hazardous and often impossible.

Captain Williamson's first undertaking was the construction of a great highway through his lands from south-east to north-west, the first of many subsequent roadways fanning out. This work was finished in 1793 and then he proceeded to establish the town of Bath on the Cohocton river. Charles says in his report that the area reminded him of the old town of Bath in Somerset but it was also thought that the town was named partly as a compliment to one his patrons and employers, William Pulteney, whose daughter had recently been created Baroness Bath.

He erected a large log-house and brought his family to stay. It is from here over the next eight years he built up the area. Many separate holdings were formed within its borders, townships created, innumerable houses built, and schools set up. Courts of Justice were established, banks opened, mills erected and every avenue to markets opened up. These with other improvements to infrastructure increased the value of the property in his care.

In "*Charles Williamson; a Review of his life*" published in 1899 William Main wrote:

> "The pioneers of civilisation have long since cut their way through the pathless forest. The ringing axe has cleared the broad valley of its oaks and pines. The denizens of the forest have been exterminated. The crowning glory of the hilltops is gone. And where Nature reigned in wild unconquered splendour the strong hand of civilisation has produced an ordered beauty. The wilderness and the solitary place have given place to rich harvest fields; the pathless forest has become a town of broad streets and spacious squares, with highways leading to other centres of civilised life and activity; where once the tall trees waved, churches and schools and stately mansions now stand; the busy hum of industry ascends where only the sounds of nature's solitude might have been heard; and men of intellect and energy, and skill, with fair women, and merry children, live and rejoice there in the prosperity that has crowned the arduous, patient, and heroic labours of the man who laid the foundation of it all."

However, difficulties arose between Charles and his backers and the result was that in 1801 he resigned his post. It was said that there was a disagreement about the finances but it was also suggested that his departure may have been hastened by the British Diplomatic Service who wanted him to work for them. He was asked to take on a special commission to Egypt, which was then run by Britain, to investigate the affairs of the country. For his report of the mission he was publicly thanked in the House of Commons. Notwithstanding that it did not always portray him in a good light, its integrity was acknowledged by the Pasha of Egypt, who presented him with a jewelled sword.

In 1805 he was sent by William Pitt with sealed orders to Admiral Lord Collingwood who was Nelson's partner at the battle of Trafalgar off Cadiz. He returned with the promise of an appointment of Governor of one of Britain's colonial dependencies. Before this, however, he was sent to Cuba in the West Indies on a Diplomatic mission. Tragically, on the return voyage he contacted yellow fever and died and he was buried at sea aged fifty one.

After his death in 1808, his widow returned to Geneva, Ontario, a town at the northern end of Seneca Lake which had been founded by her husband in 1794, and there she died in 1824.

About the author: Robert Paul was born in Dumbarton in 1845. He was ordained and inducted into the Free Church in Coldstream in 1870. In 1878 he came to Dollar where he was the Minister of the West Free Church for 32 years, until his death in 1910. Having a great interest in history he researched local topics and wrote many articles for the *Dollar Magazine*, particularly a series on the ministers of Dollar from the earliest times.

An Incident of the Desert

By H W Christie

Dollar Magazine Vol. XVI No. 61 – March 1917

Day after day, week after week, this cruel scorching heat, this monotonous existence in a camp in the desert, truly it was enough to make even stout-hearted men like these British Tommies "fed up" with everything. Each man of them longed intensely for a shower of rain, but having learned by experience that this longing was rather a waste of energy, they now very sensibly devoted their leisure hours to gazing at photographs or pictures with waterfalls, lakes, or seaside resorts depicted thereon. One of the boys possessed a *chef d'oeuvre*. It had been passed from hand to hand and gazed upon by yearning eyes until it had grown disreputable, so that now the owner would produce it on very important occasions only. It was a snapshot of a London street: rain was falling, and everything looked beautifully soaked, while through the mistiness caused by the rain the lights of this corner of London could be seen shining dimly.

A cheerful bustle was now going on all over the Fort for, Allah be praised, it was evening, and the sun had gone down. It almost seemed to have watched for a chance when no one was looking, and then dropped down quickly behind the mosque-like architecture of the Fort. When one has reached the stage of classifying old Father Sol as one of the enemy, there is no beauty in the spectacle of a sunset in the desert, and there is a great deal of sense in what a slightly sunstroked Tommy remarked when he noticed that the sun had slunk into ambush somewhere behind the camp: "I bet you it's a sham; watch " 'im bobbing up agin."

The bustle in and around the Fort increased, and two aeroplanes, each carrying an officer and mechanic, were in readiness to go up on reconnoitring work, out towards D----, where the enemy was supposed to be. These aerial scouts now set off, and to the watchers from the Fort soon appeared mere specks on the sky line.

For many a long aerial mile the aeroplanes scouted over the desert, and still nothing had been discovered of the whereabouts of the elusive enemy. Still further into the desert they went, until their stock of petrol had become alarmingly depleted. Accordingly, many miles from camp they had to descend and hold an inspection of their petrol store. It was found that there was just enough to enable one machine to reach the Fort, and so the tanks of the homeward bound aeroplane were filled, and the remaining store transferred from the other ship.

On their arrival at the Fort, the two airmen lost no time in telling of the plight of their two comrades, and the Camel Corps was at once sent off to bring in the stranded airmen and their machine. When but a score of miles from the place in which the aeroplane was lying, three of the camels collapsed through want of water, and one of the men died from exposure, and thus, as in so many other cases of relief parties which got to within several miles of the men they sought, this expedition had to return unsuccessful to the Fort. When the news of the failure of this first relieving force was brought to the camp, the C.O. moved heaven and earth in an attempt to reach the poor airmen. Aeroplanes, motor cars, cycles, dispatch riders on horses and in armoured cars were sent out in every direction. Herculean efforts were made to reach the stranded airmen, but when on the fourth day of the search the aeroplane was found, both men had disappeared, and not a sign was there to show what had happened to them. The search was persevered in, and on the evening of the fifth day both airmen were found, dead by the ----'s armoured car section.

30

The mechanic had kept a diary, the last entry in which had been written just before he died. The gist of these little pages of tragedy is this.

Weary of waiting on the relief party, and no longer able to endure the thought of another day of inactivity, the mechanic and his pilot had wandered away from the machine, possessed of some wild idea of reaching the Fort or falling in with the relief men. They wandered aimlessly on and on, getting further away from the machine and help, until in despair they found that they were quite lost in the trackless waste, and had no idea in which direction to turn to reach their machine again. Perhaps the relief party was already there, at their machine. The thought gave them fresh energy. But after covering mile after mile of sandy waste and coming no nearer their aeroplane, they lost all hope, and knew that unless the relief party reached them within a few hours, then their days on earth were numbered. Their water supply was diminishing pitifully. There was perhaps enough to keep one of them alive until help came, but when divided by two, would last out merely a few hours.

Why should two men die, when by a sacrifice on the part of one the other should be saved?

That evening, after the sun had gone down, the officer went a little way into the desert. In the cool of the evening life was doubly sweet, but the thought of another parching day, during which he would be drinking the water that spelt life for the other man, brushed aside any hesitation he may have had. A few minutes later a shot rang out – and Britain had lost another hero.

The precious water lasted the mechanic two days, at the end of which there was still no sign of the relief party. And now began for him that was left the most cruel of all tortures, that of dying of thirst in the desert. In a last despairing endeavour to slake that awful thirst, the mechanic broke his spirit level and drank the fluid. He died shortly afterwards, for this was the last entry in the diary, and when his body was found by the relief men his watch was still ticking away merrily.

They were buried in the desert, these two airmen. I have a photo of their lonely grave before me as I write. Round the base of the mound are white stones like large pebbles, while a row of smaller pebbles defines the summit. A little white cross has been laid on the top of the mound, and a tiny headstone merely tells who is buried here, adding that they died "In honour's cause."

A Night March in the Eastern Transvaal

By Keppel Harvey

Dollar Magazine Vol. II No. 5 – March 1903

The column was lying at a small station called Pan, fifteen miles east of Middelburg, the chief town in the Eastern Transvaal. It numbered 800 all told, and its strength was made up as follows:- 350 infantry, 300 cavalry, 80 artillerymen, with two 15-pounder guns, 20 men of the A.S.C. (Army Service Corps), 25 native scouts, and a pom-pom section composed of one gun and 20 men. Colonel Urmston of the Argyll and Sutherland Highlanders was in command. A column is, or always should be, prepared for a sudden march. At 7 p.m. on the 18th February 1902 we received urgent orders to move on a place situated in the Steelpoort Valley, where a party of Boers was reported to be encamped. Active preparations were set on foot, every one and everything being in readiness to move by 8 P.M. The cavalry took the lead, closely followed by three companies of infantry and two 15-pounders, each of which was drawn by six powerful horses. The transport waggons, with their teams of mules, escorted by a company of infantry, brought up the rear. As the column advanced out on the open veldt it assumed the shape of a giant serpent, and could be seen twisting its way round the numerous koppies which are scattered over the rough and stony ground. The cavalry and scouts rode in extended order, about a hundred yards ahead of the main body, and also protected the flanks of the column. About eight miles were covered when a halt was ordered. During that three hours' march not a word was spoken above a whisper, and strict orders were issued against the lighting of matches. By this time the moon was well up in the sky, and many thanks are due to it for saving men from falling into antbear holes and over ant hills.

During the halt it was curious to see the different attitudes taken up by the men. Some lay full length on the dew-covered veldt, others used their rifles as supports, and the cavalrymen passed their arms through their bridles and leant on the horses' sides. Time pressed, so we were soon on the move again, threading our way over rough ground and across several drifts.

From the rising ground an interesting view was seen. Far in the distance like so many dots the scouts were carefully picking their way, ever on the alert for hidden Boer snipers, who at this time infested the country. The long, silent, snake-like column moving over the veldt lent a peculiar and almost weird finish to the scene. The irregular line made by this cavalcade was fully two and a half miles long. The moon disappeared at 3 a.m., then it was necessary to be very careful lest a mishap, such as any one stumbling, should cause a rifle to go off. The darkness, however, did not last long, dawn breaking about 4 a.m. By this time some poor fellows were sore and weary, and scarcely able to drag one foot after the other. Every one was wondering when the object of the march would be reached. It was not long before it became apparent that something was going to happen. The cavalry was split into two parties, one going east and the other west. The infantry with the guns marched straight on. As soon as the sun rose the Steelpoort Valley was seen stretching for miles ahead, and the object of the expedition was evidently concealed in one of the kloofs in which the valley abounds.

A halt was called until a small party advanced to a line of koppies to find out the best mode of attack. In a very short time orders were issued for the immediate occupation of several commanding positions. The guns were placed at either end of the koppies. When these had been reached a very striking scene unfolded itself. About five hundred yards below, in a ravine, a large party of Boers was exposed to view, evidently unaware of the immediate presence of any enemy. They were not, however, suffered to remain long in ignorance, as a volley from the north side of the ravine showed that the cavalry had succeeded in getting round the enemy's rear. Firing now became general, and new life was instilled in the men, who a few minutes before seemed thoroughly worn out.

The Boers quickly availed themselves of the cover afforded by some rocks, and if not completely hemmed in, it is questionable if they would have given in as soon as they did. The fight while it lasted was fierce. The pom-pom, big gun, and musketry fire was telling in its effect, and succeeded in dislodging the enemy, who soon found the hopelessness of their position. The handkerchief of questionable colour, known as the white flag, was probably the most welcome sight witnessed since the march commenced. As the Boers were in force, and cases of misuse of this emblem of peace had occurred before, the Colonel took all necessary precautions, and satisfied himself that this was no ruse on the part of his wily foes to induce his men to forsake their cover. An advance party interviewed the enemy at close quarters, and took charge of their arms, ammunition, horses, stores, and provisions. Officers and men were pleased with the capture, which consisted of 189, sixteen of whom were wounded. Whilst collecting the equipment of the enemy, nine dead bodies were found and buried. That plain funeral service, where Briton and Boer stood together with uncovered heads, drew any ill-feeling from the heart and showed the logic of that seemingly paradoxical expression, "My friend the enemy."

The ground on which the fight took place was unsuitable for encamping, as a sufficient supply of water could not be obtained. The march was therefore continued to a spot two and a half miles further on. Several fellows unable to continue were helped on to transport waggons. The sun was now making itself felt, and if it had not been that the camping ground could be seen, several more of the men would have fallen out and taken their chance of being picked up by a passing waggon. On the arrival of the column at its temporary resting-place, the waggons containing the men's bivouacs were sought out and the blanket shelters quickly erected. General satisfaction was expressed that the march had not been in vain. It had lasted from 8 p.m. till 8.30 a.m., and the distance covered was 26½ miles. Fifteen minutes after the camp had been formed only the sentries and those on duty were awake, the remainder enjoying a well-earned rest. Lord Kitchener, on receipt of the news of the capture, telegraphed his congratulations to the column.

Chapter Two

Miss Christie's Travels

Miss CHRISTIE.

<u>Miss Christie of Cowden</u>

Isabella Robertson Christie, known as Ella, inherited Cowden Castle and estate in 1902. She was an intrepid traveller and the places she visited included Samarkand, India, Kashmir, Malaya, China, Korea and Japan. She was the first European woman to visit Tibet. In 1907 she conceived the idea of turning a boggy field at Cowden into a Japanese Garden. With the help of Japanese designers and gardeners, this became her life's work and it was hailed as 'the best Japanese garden in the Western World.' Unfortunately the garden was destroyed by vandals after her death and there is now little to be seen of its Japanese features.

Notes on my Travels

SHANGHAI

By Miss Christie of Cowden

Dollar Magazine Vol. VI No. 22 – June 1907

After many weeks journeying in perils of waters, what a joyful sensation is experienced when one feels the vessel firmly anchored at last, and a fresh country waiting to be explored; more especially when that country is China, whose history and civilisation are lost in the midst of antiquity, and in point of size is as large as Europe, with a fourth of the population of that continent. For several hundred miles, the mud of its greatest river, the Yangszekiang, has been carried out to sea and renders navigation extremely perilous from the numerous shoals and sand-banks to be avoided. Soon launches and sampans, or native boats, crowd alongside the stately Norddeutscher vessel, and in one of the former we embark, to steam up the tributary river Whangpoo for twelve miles in order to reach Shanghai, one of the most important commercial cities of the East. At the mouth of the river is Woosung, consisting of a collection of huts, and a railway station; the line in connection with which was made from Shanghai in 1874, then torn up by the Chinese in some of their riots, and relaid in 1898. The natives now patronise it, but European passengers usually prefer to land by steam launch.

The shores of the river are flat, with thatched huts all along a cultivated coast. A further sign of inhabitants was seen in a massive Chinese coffin on the shore waiting for burial till all the omens should be favourable for this. Thicker and thicker becomes the river traffic, a throng of vessels from all parts of the world both on peaceful and on warlike missions. Here are two white painted gunboats taken from the Spaniards and now flying the American flag; there are English, French, and German of similar kind to protect the interests and concessions of their respective countries. All treaty ports in China are thus divided, but it by no means follows that the lines are as sharply drawn regarding the inhabitants. The Chinese themselves, in Shanghai, swarm in the English concession, and to guard the varied nations the police force consist of Sikhs with their red turbans, the familiar English "bobby" and the Chinese with his pig-tail, a trio which may frequently be observed controlling the miscellaneous traffic and quite succeeding in keeping order amid such a chaos. The settlements in Shanghai are laid out according to the respective ideas of each country. In the French settlement one finds the Chinese speaking excellent French, no pidgin language as taught and kept up by the British and the streets are called "rue" although a projected one bears the name "Avenue Ferguson", we imagine from some Franco-Scottish feeling.

The Bund is the great promenade along the river-bank, and, laid out with gardens and avenues of trees, forms a promenade that would do credit to any town in East or West. On one side of it are built the palatial commercial offices and clubs. The broad drive is filled with such a varied picture as to defy description. The rich, both foreign and native, bowl along in glass all-round broughams, with either two men on the box, or one of these standing on the step behind and hanging on to straps worthy of a Lord Mayor's coach. It is rather a come-down to find the vehicle drawn by only one horse, and that rather of a pony size. Sometimes, in the owner's absence I have seen the said lackey driving inside, and picking up a friend on the way. Automobiles rush along and threaten to exterminate the crowd of rickshaws with their perspiring coolies; tasselled chairs carrying richly dressed celestials; barrows with their poorer brethren, of a construction that has the wheel inside and the barrow out, like an Irish car, thus enabling four to six passengers and their many bundles to be accommodated, are trundled along by a coolie who partly supports the weight by a shoulderstrap; bicycles dart about, and coolies in pairs shout for a free passage while carrying marvellous weights slung on a bamboo pole.

The race-course of Shanghai is the finest in the East, and the meetings held there not less so, attracting visitors from as far distant as Singapore. The Chinese element gathers chiefly from the spirit of gambling rather than from the love of horse flesh, as can be understood of a people that can own and take pleasure in fighting crickets or in staking its money on a game such as "fan tan," which is simply dividing a pile of counters into fours, and betting on how many remain of the last three! There are large cotton mills on the river-bank, though curiously enough the material of the blue cotton garments worn by the natives both at Shanghai and up country is made in Lancashire and dyed by the Chinese themselves. Something like twelve millions is said to be annually imported of this commodity.

The native city of Shanghai is walled round like all other cities and villages in China, and its gates shut in a population of over 200,000, living in the narrowest of streets and under conditions such as would kill off in a short time a white race. No attempts are made at drainage, and scum and filth of every kind with rotting garbage are only cleared from the bye-ways to be flung into the stagnant ditches that intersect the city. Forty occupants are an allowance for a house that in comfort could not accommodate ten; and yet we are told that disease in an epidemic form is not more rampant than in cities where our so-called civilised ideas prevail. No wheeled traffic of any kind is possible, not even the familiar rickshaw, but one is jostled and shouted at by weight-carrying coolies, who also keep a sort of grunt to mark step as they trot along.

The shops are arranged according to their commodities in different streets, so one knows where to find goods by asking for the jade street, silk street, ivory street, and so on. In a country where bargaining is part of the trade, this is a help, as, if one cannot come to terms in one shop, another dealer is at hand who may be more desirous to sell. As a rule the dealer is honest, never going back when once he has agreed on a price; a joke of even a feeble kind always helps, and never fails to amuse the crowd of interested onlookers. The shops are open fronted, so all going on can be seen and heard; the goods are usually shown in glass cases if of a valuable nature, and the counter extends two-thirds across the opening. In the back portion of the shop is seen a table or small altar, its front hung with an embroidered square and on it are offerings of various kinds of food and drink, and incense sticks burning before the ancestral tablets.

At the Chinese New Year, commencing in the middle of February, is to be seen, even in the meanest hovel, a dish in which is grown on pebbles the Chinese New Year lily, like our narcissus, but sometimes in a dwarfed form. For a fortnight or more a time of cessation from work prevails, bills are settled, best clothes produced, and crackers, large and small, are let off day and night till the streets are a mass of their red paper fragments. Decorations are hung up, and on every dwelling, both by sea and land, are pasted orange-coloured tags of paper with black characters invoking the five chief blessings, such as wealth, long life, and many grandsons.

The shop signs are usually gilt and are oblong boards hanging down from outside the building, giving the streets a gay appearance, especially when conjoined with the elaborately carved and gilt fronts of the higher class tradesmen's stores. Food shops abound all through the native city, and also perambulating cook-shops where hot food can be obtained of quite an appetising nature. There are also stalls where the raw article is in demand in the form of sweet potatoes, pink turnip-looking lumps, sugar cane in lengths, or water chestnuts resembling lily bulbs. The higher class restaurants are hung with brown-glazed pigs, flattened out ducks with necks drawn out like swans, fowls cooked whole even to their combs, and dried rats with curly tails, these last supposed to enhance the keenness of vision. One fails to see the train of reasoning, which seems farther fetched than another instance I heard of which had more to recommend it. A Chinaman, in attendance on an Englishman who had just killed a hawk, at once picked out the eyes of the bird for his wife to swallow as pills to cure the blindness that afflicted her.

The original of the willow pattern tea house is in the heart of the city, a wooden building erected in the centre of a stagnant pool and approached by a zigzag bridge of granite slabs; an offering made by a Chinaman five hundred years ago to expiate a sin he had unwittingly committed against God and the "Sun of the World", his Emperor. The building is kept up by his descendants, and when necessary renewed in parts exactly as in the original, even to the tint of the wood. The style of our so-called restoration of old buildings would not be tolerated in China. One feature of the city life is the close proximity of the habitations of the rich to those of the poor, only that the former isolate themselves by a wall all round their demesne. Suddenly, out of an indescribable noise and crowd one passes through a heavily guarded portal into a haven of peace. Summer-houses, with windows glazed with pearl shells giving a delicately tinted light, and grottoes are found among the rock work, which is built up to imitate hill scenery in miniature; through it paths are laid out, and climb up and down in twistings and turnings so as to far surpass the windings of the Maze at Hampton Court. Miniature lakes and rivers are crossed by bridges, and the coping of the wall is formed in snake-like undulations with dragon head and tail. The Chinaman in charge took the greatest delight in displaying the intricacies of his garden, and the more we begged to be let out the less he heeded. "One more picey chop, chop" had such a horribly realistic suggestion about it, considering that at the entrance we had been shown the execution ground with gory stains, and one Frenchman of the party consolingly exclaimed "Mais jamais ils ne nous permettront de sortir, je vais dire mes prières" Their escape having been made, there remained still to be seen the fortune-tellers that, for a fraction of penny, would tell a fortune from the hand; and the story-tellers surrounded by an interested crowd of listeners as they retailed their traditional stock.

The Confucian temples are crowded with devotees, both men and women who bring their offerings of food and candles or joss-sticks, kneel down and say a prayer, then toss for luck as to their chief object on hand, and from the favourable or unfavourable sign deduct a guidance.

Foreigners are not stared at as a rule but rather passed over in utter contempt, the Chinaman being conscious of his superiority in point of centuries as a nation, and of his possession of the earliest known civilisation.

Notes on my Travels

THE BALEARIC ISLANDS

By Miss Christie of Cowden

Dollar Magazine Vol. X No. 37 – 1911

Why, where are they? And what is there to see? In the West Indies, are they not? were some of the questions that met my proposal of going to the Balearic Islands. In reply I can only state that they are neither in the West Indies nor in the Grecian Archipelago, but are a group of islands in the Mediterranean off the coast of Spain, of which the principal ones are Majorca, Minorca, Iviza, and Fortunera. That there is much of interest to see in them may well be believed when one realises that their known history extends back many centuries. Exploited by the Romans in their marvellous sweeping conquests, one still finds traces of their occupation succeeding those of the Phoenicians and Carthaginians. In Port Mahon we find perpetuated the name of Mago, brother of Hannibal 206 B.C., and the Roman Consul, Gaius Cecillius Metellus was surnamed Balearicus in honour of his conquest of the islands, where he founded the towns of Palma and Pollentia.

Subsequently the Vandals, the Romans of the Eastern Empire, the Moors, and Jaime I of Aragon ruled in turn. At one time the islands had even the distinction of being an independent kingdom, but were definitely united to Aragon in the fourteenth century. Minorca was for a time in the hands of the British, but was given up in the peace of 1802, and now all the islands form a province of Spain, administered over by a Captain-General, resident in Palma. The inhabitants, numbering some 350,000, are an industrious people, speaking Catalan dialect, and are engaged in vine and fruit culture and farming pursuits. The island of Majorca is mapped out in the flatter and richer districts like a continuous orchard, and in early spring there can be few more beautiful sights than the blossom-laden trees bending over acres of sweet-scented beans, with which the fields are thickly sown. Mingled with those are fields for the culture of the olive, and its grey green colouring blends softly with the pink colouring of the peach and almond. Grotesque to the last degree are the shapes of those olive trees, and their distorted forms are suggestive of the freaks of a Barnum's show. "Many of the old trees stand on a kind of tripod formed by the splitting and shrinking of their own trunk: here a hoary veteran of many centuries has wound himself into an excellent imitation of a corkscrew; a group of twisted crones appears to gossip together with uplifted hands, while two sprawling wrestlers are locked as in a death struggle in each other's arms. Here squats a gnarled mass like nothing so much as a gigantic toad; there a boa constrictor twines itself in folds about its prey, and an antediluvian monster stoops to examine with interest the strange human insect that has adventured itself within reach."

In addition to purely agricultural pursuits the Majorcans are also expert shoemakers, and I seldom saw a town with more boot shops than Palma, possibly the cobble-paved streets give good trade, although the native country foot covering is a grass sandal, or a plaited jute sole with canvas uppers, which are at the same time both practical and comfortable and give foothold in rocky climbs. A legacy from the Moors is the manufacture of Majolica ware, especially tiles, with which the steps of staircases are faced. The designs of many are Arabic in character and in colouring resemble those of Spain. Lace making and most exquisite embroidery on linen, basket weaving, and the plaiting of string seats and backs of chairs are all carried on in Palma and other country towns. The making of silver chain purses and bags is largely carried on for export trade, as are also minute silver charms, and gold and silver chains are measured off and sold by the palm on which to hang the attractive enamel peasant jewellery pendants.

The Majorcans are a most courteous people, honest, industrious, and noted for their good looks. Begging is hardly ever met with, and they are always ready to help a stranger even to the extent of shouting directions in his ear, should he fail to understand Mallorquin, and even to take his part against a native should occasion arise, as the following little incident will show. On a driving tour through the island I had arranged the exact route with a driver, and the last day, for some unknown reason, to me at least, he declined to take it. We argued for some time fruitlessly, and he and the "padrone" followed me upstairs when I bolted the door and bade them be gone. When I judged by the sound of their retreating steps that they had disappeared, I sailed forth and searched the town till I found a diligence, and engaged a place in it to return by the desired route. I then told the driver his services could now be dispensed with and paid him what was due. He tossed the money down along with his tip. This last I removed and barricaded myself in my room. In a short time more steps approached, and, looking out, found the driver accompanied by a *gens d'armes* (corresponding to our policeman). I signed to him to come in and shut the door, as I could not sit in a draught. It was difficult to maintain a dignified position, as owing to the onslaught of mosquitoes the previous night, both my eyes were almost closed, and I sat mopping them with a cooling lotion while the *gens d'armes* and I conversed in Spanish, and the driver explained the cause of my sufferings. The *gens d'armes* was most sympathetic and hoped the lotion would do good, and what was of more use, took my part entirely as to the route, - this in spite of the driver reiterating that he was *his* friend. The whole scene was like a play, and we parted the best of friends, the driver hurried out to countermand the seat in the diligence, and he and the "padrone" assisted me in bargaining for a water jar. These water jars are made both in pottery and copper, and are of classic shapes as the guidebooks say, no kerosene tins or enamelled iron are in use in the country districts, and in the evening one meets crowds of women balancing those amphorae jars on their heads as they return from the wells or fountains. Water of excellent quality is pumped up by windmills which are a great feature in the landscape, or else it is drawn from wells. Light wine is universally drunk, being both cheap and good and not so acid as the country wines of France. Little meat is used unless pork, vegetables, bread, oil, and eggs being the staple diet. The houses are stone built, the masons of Majorca being famed as builders, especially dry stone work which is like mosaic, so well are the stones jointed. The doorways and windows of the houses have each a band of whitewash round them which brightens the brown expanse of stone and lime. Glass is not extensively used, a wooden shutter with perhaps a pane of glass, or two at most, inserted in the upper half. Ploughing is done by a very primitive wooden implement, and the grubbing is completed by droves of black pigs, long-legged creatures with floppy ears, and it is a common sight in the evening to meet them being driven home by the children. Education is not compulsory, so school hours have not to be considered, and the children can thus help in many ways as well as those connected with farming. Many of the farm-houses were formerly known as Possession-houses, and were originally the country seats of the Spanish nobility; but the great land-owners no longer reside in their ancestral homes, which are handed over to the principal tenant on the estate who goes by the name of the Amo or Master. Most picturesque and spacious are many of these old buildings, their vast apartments scantily furnished with remnants of past glory and their walls still bearing the scutcheon of some noble founder.

The country inns are primitive but always clean, with brick floors. There are no fireplaces except in the kitchen for cooking purposes, and the fuel used is not such as would roast an ox, sometimes it is reduced to a handful of almond shells. On one occasion when storm-stayed by heavy snow showers in the mountains and rain in the plains, how ineffectual was the heat afforded by a brazier, when the circle was large and seven or eight chilly individuals gathered round it. The landlord being the possessor of three sons, one had married a year previously to "quite an heiress" as was whispered to me with pride, "600 pesetas (about £40) was her *dot*," but thrown in with this was vilest squint I have ever had the misfortune to look at; however, she seemed amiable and very proud of her three-day-old baby, while she caressingly kept turning up the tip of its little button nose. In right of her 600 pesetas and the baby, she had the warmest seat round the brazier and the tit-bits from the family meals, and to cheer the party, her husband, an enthusiast in music, though entirely self-taught, thundered out the most stirring Wagner melodies on a tin-kettle of a piano that lacked the ivories of three white keys, and was uncertain about two of the blacks. That "living room" is a memory.

Notes on My Travels

SEOUL, COREA

By Miss Christie of Cowden

Dollar Magazine Vol. VIII No. 30 – June 1909

The people seem intelligent, and there seems to be a general awakening among them from their conservative ideas. A court lady has started a medical school for female students, and I was present at the first women's conference for the promotion of female education. The chairman, a lady, the only one dressed in European costume, spoke French, and rapped with her mallet on the table to keep order. The meeting was packed to overflowing by an interested crowd, but I was somewhat sorry to hear that another object of the meeting was for the abolition of the native dress in favour of a European style. The ladies' palanquins were waiting in rows upon rows for them outside, and also a dense crowd of men who seemed to share the general excitement such a meeting had produced.

The royal palace has quite an imposing entrance; a very broad roadway lined with different official buildings leads up to the main gate. The ex-Emperor no longer inhabits or even sees it, as he never goes out for fear of being murdered. The Empress was murdered in 1894 "by the Japanese," say the Coreans. She was a clever woman who loved her country, and hated the Japanese, so a soldier climbed over the wall one fine day and cut her to bits in a room of the north palace, removed the bits to the garden and there buried them. The Coreans did not know of this for years, but terror of the same fate sent the ex-Emperor hurrying in hot haste in a palanquin to the Russian Legation, where he has remained ever since, and Marquis

Ito reigns in his stead. Both the winter and summer palaces consist of many pavilions built of wood, carved and decorated. The walls of the various rooms are made of light frames of wood lined with oiled paper, and the size of the rooms can be determined according to the position of the screens which are slid into grooves in the floor. In this way a thousand rooms could be made in the summer palace. In hot weather these screens are hung from the ceiling, and the air allowed to circulate the whole length of the building. The summer palace was built six hundred years ago, and has not been inhabited for a hundred and fifty years. It is beautifully situated in the midst of parks and woods many miles in extent, but it is sad to see the once cared for buildings fast crumbling to ruin, and the terraced gardens, planted with such care and adorned with what was no doubt regarded as of special value, namely blocks of fossil wood set in large richly-carved stone pots, so neglected.

The variety of pines is great, and in every direction there is always the background of lovely hills rising so suddenly as to give almost a stage effect. The dress of both men and women is white cotton, which has a somewhat chilly effect in cold weather, though quilted clothing is often worn when additional warmth is required. The women of Seoul wear, hanging on their heads, a long, bright green silk coat which has a charming effect of colouring. Its origin dates from about 1500, during a memorable attack on the town, made when many of the men were absent. The women covered themselves with the men's coats to deceive the enemy, and led the defence; and they have ever since worn this badge of their bravery. The little girls, in rose-coloured petticoats down to their heels, and bright green silk bodices, are very attractive, merry little people, and seem not to mind the burden of a baby sister or brother tied to their backs; in fact, to see any girl of ten without one would cause surprise, and even the boys are not exempt if possessed of younger brothers and sisters. Equally patient are the poor infants, who are shaken severely as their child nurses run about and play all manner of games, quite irrespective of their charges. The shops are open fronted and are often distinguished by some sign, such as a basket on the end of a pole to denote a wine shop or a flag for a pawnbroker.

The method of bread-making is not appetising, carried on as it is in the midst of the dusty or muddy roadway. The dough is laid on a board on the ground, and two men set to work with large wooden mallets to beat it time about. The mallets are afterwards laid on the roof of the house as the lowness of the walls makes it a convenient shelf on which to lay anything. Washing of clothes is done in any muddy gutter that offers sufficient flow of water to wet them. Then much beating and pounding on stones is required, and the same treatment is pursued by way of mangling or ironing. The damp garment is placed on a sloping slab of stone, and on it is placed a wooden roller which is hammered round and round upon the article being dressed, which is sadly detrimental to the garment.

The men's hats are a striking feature, both their summer and winter ones. The latter are somewhat the shape of the old high-crowned Welsh hat, and are made of finely split bamboo and horsehair lacquered black all over, and are tied on under the chin with a strip of folded horsehair canvas. Instead of an umbrella a fan-shaped piece of oilcloth is carried and when un-folded exactly covers the hat, and it also is tied under the chin.

The general appearance of Corea is mountainous, with extensive plains on which rice is cultivated. It is also well wooded in parts, chiefly pines and firs of different species, and in spring a lovely pink azalea is to be seen amongst the copse wood of the hillsides. Pinzang is the ancient capital of the country and is a fairly large town composed of mud huts with thatched roofs. There are a few superior buildings and a so-called palace, which if ever it had deserved the name in the usual sense of the word, it hardly does so now, as it is almost demolished with the exception of an ancient wall. Great preparations appear to be made to rebuild it. Gigantic columns of wood are strewn about and have been for years, so my guide told me. One sort of audience hall is finished and there was great demur at letting me see it as nothing royal in Corea is allowed to be looked upon by the *canaille*.

The long, necessary delay at getting permission from the Corean officials was not repaid except in the sight of an old creature clad in crimson gauze, the official court dress. He entered into conversation by means of an interpreter and asked where I came from. He said I must be tired after such a long journey, though, as to where Scotland was, I do not suppose he had the faintest idea, and probably associated it with either the North Pole or heaven, as in giving a sketch of the world with my umbrella point on the sand, the limit of earth appeared nearly reached. There is a curious collection of royal tombs, but it was impossible to ascertain their age – anything from three thousand to three hundred. The guide started at four thousand years old, but I should question if they are even half that. The town is built on the Pyang, a broad river which runs down to Chenampo where the Russians had hoped, at one time, to make a harbour. Possibly this may now be done by the Japanese, who will no doubt do their best to develop the mineral and other wealth resources of the country, and in thus enriching themselves one hopes they will let the poor battered-about owners of the country have a share.

Chapter Three

Nature Notes

John Strachan

Dr John Strachan Jnr was educated at Dollar Academy. In 1865 he joined his father's medical practice in Dollar. His enlightened views on health, education and the causes of criminality were much in advance of their time. He was the originator of the Dollar Academy Club for former pupils, the first meeting being held in his own house. Dr Strachan was a keen naturalist, birds being his particular interest. He was also a founder and editor of the *Dollar Magazine*. He died in 1928.

J.S. It seems likely that J.S., the author of witty *The Ghost at Tait's Tomb,* was Dr John Strachan.

56

THE BIRDS OF THE DISTRICT

Our Feathered Minstrels

By J Strachan M.D.

Dollar Magazine Vol. IV No. 14 – June 1906

The Redstart, or Firetail (Silvia or Ruticilla phoenicurus). It is generally considered that among birds fine feathers and musical talent do not go together, but this scarcely holds true of the redstart. It is one of the most brightly coloured of British birds, and is one of the most attractive when seen flitting shyly among the trees and bushes in the quiet retirement of the Castle Glen, Vicar's Bridge, or the Cowden and Arndean woods, uttering its quaint little call of "oi-chit-chit," by which it may be readily identified. As its name will suggest – *steort* being the Saxon for tail – it is chiefly distinguished by the bright rusty red colour of its tail and tail coverts which are shown off to advantage by its pretty way of spreading out the feathers and shaking the tail with an up-and-down motion, at the same time bobbing its body after the manner of a water-crow. The bright colours are beautifully contrasted, the beak, face, and throat being black, the forehead white, the breast red, shading off into white behind; the head, neck, and back blue-grey, and the wings and two centre feathers of the tail reddish brown.

As compared with others of the warbler tribe, the song of the redstart is not of great compass, but it possesses to the full the soft liquid sweetness so characteristic of the family, and is very pleasing to listen to of a warm summer gloaming, or in the early morning. Whatever may be wanting in the song is fully made up for in the variety of pretty vocalism in which the bird indulges, closely resembling, it is said, the notes of the sparrow, the chaffinch, the garden-warbler, and the lesser whitethroat. In captivity the redstart may be *taught* to sing any tune which is whistled to it, but when we consider the amount of patient persistence and isolation required to effect this, we can scarcely suppose that such imitation takes place under natural conditions and surroundings. As in the case of the starling, such resemblances are, I believe, only coincidences, the particular notes being as natural to the one bird as to the other. Altogether the singing and warbling of the redstart, along with the beautiful colouring and sprightly ways of the bird, afford a treat well worth the exercise of patience and self-restraint necessary to avoid alarming a somewhat timid nature, and are a worthy object for an evening stroll in the localities mentioned, or an early rise of a May morning.

The hen redstart is not very particular as to where she builds her nest, so long as it is well hidden in some hole or hollow in a bank, or old wall, in the stump of a tree, or even in a conveniently placed flower-pot or watering-can. Two which I have seen in recent years were placed simply among the herbage of a bank by the roadside - one in the Castle Wynd near the Gloomhill quarry, the other just beyond Linbank farm – the whereabouts in each case being pretty clearly indicated by the distressful agitation and alarm notes of the male bird on guard among the branches of a neighbouring tree, while his mate was sitting close upon her eggs, leaving them only on our very near approach. The nest is composed of moss, dry grass and leaves rather closely put together, and lined with hair and feathers. The eggs are usually five in number, and of a uniform light greenish blue colour, much like those of the hedge sparrow or dunnock, but smaller, and of a paler shade of blue.

The Stonechat (Silvia rubicola) is another very handsome, brightly coloured member of this family, from the rest of which he differs in being of a more hardy nature, thus not requiring to leave us during the winter, but only to seek the milder and more sheltered parts of his native land. The summer habitat of the stonechat is in waste and stony places, as in the pass leading by Maiden's Well to Glenquey, up to the Bank Burn and along the Dunning road, where his bright and striking appearance, sprightly ways, and peculiar "chack-chack" note do much to enliven the scene. His personality can scarcely be mistaken if once seen. The whole of the head and neck are black mottled with dark blue, the breast of a rich bright orange shading off into white towards the tail; the shoulders and tail coverts white, with a dash of white upon each wing; the back and wing coverts dark reddish brown mottled with black, and the wings and tail brown streaked with red – all of which, combined with a handsome figure, and restless, pretty way of flitting from stone to stone, alighting upon the topmost branch of a bush of shrub, or hovering in space a little way above it, hanging on to the bending stem of some reed or plant, and flitting to the ground for a moment and back again to some more elevated perch, all the time flirting the tail and dipping the body, so displaying to the full the bright adornment which Nature has lavished upon him, form an object well worth looking out for in our walks about the hills. The stonechat is not at all common in the district; frequenting out-of-the-way places, and usually to be seen only singly or in pair, it is very apt to escape the notice of the "stay at home" and the unobservant. It is, however, quite one of the tit-bits of Nature which we may hope to come across in suitable localities. His usual note, as the name implies, is like the clacking of two stones together, but he has also got a pretty little song of his own, soft, low and sweet, and peculiarly welcome in the lonely places he loves. It must be listened for, however, to be enjoyed, or it may be lost amid the bubbling ripple of the burn and the sough of the Ochil breeze among the bracken of the hillside.

Long before the other warblers have ventured home from their winter sojourn in the sunny south, the stonechats have entered upon the serious business of nesting. About the end of March or the beginning of April the happy pair have made their domestic arrangements for the season, have, after much deliberation and anxious quest, fixed upon a suitable site at the bottom of or in the heart of a whin bush, to which even a schoolboy would think twice or many times before he ventured to penetrate; and there, with bits of moss, dry grass, root fibres, &c., built a roomy, substantial nest, and lined it cosily with hair and feathers. Then come the eggs, five or six in number, of a pale greenish blue colour with the larger end speckled with small reddish brown spots. Upon these the mother bird, in sober garb as compared with the male so as not to attract attention, settles warmly and tenderly down to her long, loving vigil; while he keeps watch and guard outside, cheering her with his song, and giving timely warning, should danger approach, by his loud, sharp alarm note "chack-chack-chack," when, if necessary, she will slip gently off and flit warily among the bushes to a little distance before showing herself, that she may afford no indication of where her treasures lie.

The Whinchat (Silvia or Praticola rubitra) – What would the Dunning road be without the whinchat and wheatear? Well, it would scarcely be the Dunning road as we love to think of it of a warm summer's day, when the rock rose is hanging in yellow tassels from the rock near the bridge; when white festoons of trailing saxifrage and gem-like clusters of dainty primrose deck the dripping crags on the right, with the brawling burn on our left, as we begin the ascent of the Greenneuk Brae; when the Dunning Moss is ablaze with the delicate pale yellow of the globe flower, the rich golden-hued marsh marigold, and the feathery pink and white spike of the bog-bean; and when the Queigh Burn is gay with the beautiful mimulus flower, bedecking every jutting rock, islet stone, and patch of gravel, amid the bright sparkle, the crystal clear ripple and splash of the rushing water, all in a setting of the richest green. These are all there as well as the lovely rolling slopes of the hills on either side; but where, we would ask, looking about with unsatisfied gaze, where are the beautiful little birds that used to accompany us by the road-side, flitting along from post to post of the wire fence and seeming to enjoy and welcome our society? The heart and soul would seem to have gone out of the scene, leaving a blank which would take greatly from our enjoyment of it. But, thank our stars, and the remoteness of the scene from egg-collecting schoolboys! We have to mourn no such loss, for here they are this bright May day, as plentiful and as friendly as ever. The whinchat has but lately arrived from winter quarters, and has lost no time in seeking out the loved native home among the Ochils. The male is a beautiful little bird in both form and colouring, and is not so shy but that we may get a good view as he alights for a few moments on the fence within a dozen yards of us. The head and cheeks are dark brown mottled with black, but with a broad pure white band above each eye, reaching from the beak to nearly the back of the head; the throat is white, the breast pale orange shading off to yellowish white underneath; the back is brown, spotted all over with black; the wings are dark brown, the wing coverts edged with a lighter shade and a white band at the upper part; the tail feathers are pure white tipped for about a third of their length with greyish black; and the legs and feet black, the colours being all as if laid on and touched in with the most perfect artistic skill and with charming effect. Its motions, too, are in keeping with the neat, sprightly little figure and pretty colouring. On our first approach it flits along before us, uttering its peculiar note of "peep-tic-tic-tic-tic" on alighting with a dainty shake of the tail and raising of the wings; then off, perhaps, to another post a few yards farther on, or to a stone or whin bush on the hillside, and so on from point to point, repeating its alarm note as we follow it up. But if we are not in a hurry, and have patience to dismount and take a seat quietly for ten or fifteen minutes – and in this warm sunshine, and amid such surroundings, it is a very agreeable thing to do, even without the soothing influence of a pipe – we may be rewarded by seeing him in the full enjoyment of a happy and cheery disposition, now perched upon a bending twig watching with head coquettishly turned to the side for the passing fly which he will pursue and capture on the wing, or darting down among the herbage to pick up a caterpillar which his sharp eye has detected just emerging from a sheltering leaf; then off, with nimble flit of wing and pretty flirt of the tail, to a neighbouring bush, where, alighting on the extremity of a slender twig which bends beneath his weight, he gives vent to his sweet, melodious little song which he continues, as, springing lightly into the air, he hovers on fluttering wing and outspread tail for a few seconds before returning to his perch. Now he is joined by his similarly but less brightly coloured spouse and some pretty love passages with shuffling wings and mutual "chat-chat" and loving little twitterings are indulged in; then the two fly off to yon whin bush by the roadside, alighting on the topmost twigs, but presently darting underneath to examine the spot at its root which she has selected as suitable for the nest about to be built. Let us not go near it at present, as they would be easily scared, but note the spot, and we may return a fortnight hence and have a look. It will be no easy matter, even with the knowledge now acquired, to find the nest, which will be carefully hidden and cleverly assimilated to the withered grass and whin twigs under the bush; nor need we expect any help from the actions of the mother bird, who is very cunning in leaving the nest even when alarmed, slipping quietly off her eggs and threading her way through the bush to emerge on quite the other side. Trusting to the natural shelter in which it is placed, the whinchat is not very particular in building the nest, which is large, about six inches across, though only two and a half inches internally, and rather loosely put together. It is composed, externally, of stalks of grass and moss, and lined with fine blades of withered grass, with perhaps a little wool or hair. The eggs are very similar in hue to the fresh whin spines through which we have to look for them, a glossy bluish green colour, and are generally five or six in number. The birds show great concern for the safety of the nest, keeping up an incessant "peep-tic-tic-tic," and doing their best by flitting along just in front to lead us from it. They are doubtless greatly relieved and very happy on their return, after we have passed on, to find their treasure intact, but why they should be in any fear may be for some of us to say. It will be worth while to pay it another visit some three weeks later to see the full fruition of their loving care and solicitude in the pretty little fledglings of mottled grey and white, which will then be tasting the first joys of a bright and sunny life. If not yet fully launched upon their aerial existence, the parent bird will be seen repeatedly alighting upon the sheltering bush or a neighbouring post, each time with some dainty morsel in its beak; and a careful watch will then reveal the little innocents timidly venture a little way into the open with fluttering wing and expectant beak, and having received their portion, immediately retire again into concealment. By the middle or end of June they are fairly on the wing, and lose all timidity in full confidence of their powers of flight, and a bright and lively time it then is on the Dunning road. In July or August a second brood may appear, and after a happy couple of months spent amid scenes of blooming heather and bright young bird life, the whole family, along with many other such families, depart for the Riviera or beyond, to avoid the dreary months of a northern winter, but to gladly return next May to their home among the Ochils.

The Wheatear (Sylvia or Saxicola aenanthe). This elegant and attractive bird is also a marked feature upon the Dunning road in spring and summer, as it is of most of the hilly parts of the district. Being among the very earliest arrivals from winter quarters, its first appearance there in the beginning of April is very welcome as a sign of returning spring and breaking up of dull deadness of the dreary winter months. Our attention may be first attracted by the bright flash of white which catches the eye, accompanied, perhaps, by a "chat-chat" as the bird seems to drop from the wall or fence on which it has been sitting, and, after flitting along near the ground for some thirty or forty yards, re-alights upon some similar eminence. It then stands very upright, showing off a very handsome figure and striking plumage, and turning its head from side to side with alert watchfulness. With care we may get near enough to see and admire the perfect taste and conspicuous design for artistic effect with which the colouring is arranged. The throat and breast are of a pale rufous brown, shading off to white near the tail; the crown of the head, the neck and the back is black, and from its base stretches a broad black band including the eye at its upper part, and extending beyond to the blue of the neck, while above and below is a margin of white. The wings and wing coverts are almost black, but each feather is edged with brownish white, or in parts, with a rich rufous brown; the upper and under tail coverts and two-thirds of the under part of the tail are black, the feathers edged with brownish white; the legs and feet are black. But no description of mine can give any adequate conception of this beautiful bird, which must be seen in its native haunts with all the grace and elegance of motion and the abounding vitality of happiness which go to make up one of the most attractive specimens of Nature's handiwork. Fortunately this no difficult matter for those residing in or visiting the Devon Valley – that is, if they are content with driving their "own pair" or with the silent, smooth running bicycle for getting about – as the wheatear is fairly plentiful and is widely distributed among the Ochils. I have even seen it on the Muckhart road down as far as Bell's Bridge. If we keep quiet we may now see him dart off from his perch with a brilliant flash of his white tail coverts, capture a fly or moth some dozen yards off, and back again to the same spot with a contented "chat-chat" as he looks smartly about for some other object of sport; or we may be fortunate enough to hear the soft, pleasant, warbling song with which he seeks to cheer his loving mate engaged in domestic duties under some big stone near by, and to see him, perhaps, hovering over the spot with flickering wings and expanded tail as he sweetly tells her of his love. Is it not enough to make us thankful for our humanity which enables us, alone of all animals, to appreciate and enjoy all this loveliness and beauty? "Oh, if we only had a gun! What a capital chance for a shot," for the bird is good to eat. We are told that countless numbers of these birds are taken every year on the Southern Downs for the table, being much esteemed as a delicacy. No humanity is needed for this. I have no doubt but that the hawk and the cat have quite as keen a relish for such "delicacy" as has the epicure of the table, and they have probably as much pleasure in tearing the life out of the bird with beak and claw as the sportsman has in "bringing it down" with his gun. Let us be thankful for the four hundred miles between the Ochils and the London market, and that the Scottish palate does not crave for such "table delicacies". I have never heard of the wheatear being shot+ or captured for the table in this district. But see! The mother bird has left her nest for fresh air and exercise, incubation not being far advanced, so, while the two are doing a little "billing and cooing" on yonder knoll, we may take the opportunity to have a look – not that we could see much with the carnal eye at the far end of that hole under the stone, but the mind's eye is subject to no such limitation. There is not much of a nest, only a quantity of dry grass laid somewhat loosely on the floor of the cave with a depression in the centre which is lined with some wool, feathers, and rabbit's fur; but there are five eggs right enough, of an elegant rather elongated form, and of a uniform delicate blue colour a little darker at the thicker end. Pretty they are to look at, but oh! the wonder of the power which dwells inside of producing, in a few short weeks under the warmth of the maternal breast, a bird in all its completeness and beauty. Let us not contemplate the degrading alternative of all that is wonderful and interesting being blown out in order that the pretty *shell* may be kept.

The wheatear may be kept in confinement, and is said then to sing very prettily by night, sometimes, as well as by day. If it be well treated and cared for, I do not see that there is any cruelty in this, and the resulting enjoyment to ourselves is certainly of a very human order. There would be lacking scope for much that is attractive in its ways, but what remains would be brought more fully within reach, and is such as to draw out our more kindly human feelings.

65

Being on the Dunning road, we cannot but mark the *Red-shank (Totanus calidris)*, already referred to under "Returning Friends," which may have been scared from her apology for a nest among a clump of rushes, on our approach to gather a few of the beautiful globe flowers or bogbean. It is, indeed, impossible to ignore her presence as she circles about us with a slow, quivering flight, her long red shanks trailing in the abandonment of grief or anxiety, occasionally swooping down as if with intent to strike us with her wings, and all the time uttering her loud, shrill, whistling note of alarm, her spouse seconding her efforts with many gesticulations, but at a higher elevation and more respectful distance, his musical "liddle-liddle-liddle" coming to us as a piteous appeal to be merciful. We may have a look at the nest before relieving the anxious parents of our dreaded presence so near their treasures. It is not much of a nest, only a little dry grass lining a slight depression among the rushes; but there are the four eggs which render it the centre of love and devotion to at least one tender little heart. They are of a pale reddish white, tinged with green, and blotted, spotted, and speckled with dark red brown mostly at the thicker end. Very pretty they are as they lie there amid their surrounding of green rushes and meadow grass, and form a picture which may remain upon the memory for a lifetime. But let us get back now to the road and watch patiently till, their fears having subsided, we can observe the birds under less exciting and distressing conditions. The mother soon ceases her cries and, impelled by the "deep sitting" stage to which the eggs have reached, to less caution than she might otherwise display, after a final wheel raises her wings to an upright position, thus showing off the beautifully white plumage underneath, and alights on a mound near. Then closing her wings, and, standing for a minute at the full stretch of her red shanks, she stoops her head and neck and walks deliberately through the rushes to her nest, profoundly thankful to find the eggs intact and not yet dangerously cool from the exposure. But here comes the male wheeling round with his rapid, strong, jerking flight, the wings never fully expanded, and now with a sweep over the meadow and a similar display of his brilliant white undergarment, he has settled near enough to allow us, with the aid of a good field glass, to examine his pretty plumage and general aspect. His long red legs and toes and moderately long red but black-tipped beak are in marked and pleasing contrast to the prevailing white of the body, throat, and face, which are more or less spotted all over with dark brown; the top of the head, the back of the neck, and the back are dark brown spotted with black, and the wings are brown are mottled with black and greyish white above, but pure white underneath. He is a handsome and graceful bird, and well repays the attention we have given to him. Now, having satisfied himself to the safety of the nest, he is off again like an arrow, cleaving the air with short powerful strokes of the wing, higher and higher, as he wheels around till he appears but a speck in the blue lift, from whence his soft musical love note "leero-leero-leero" joins with the "whaup-whaup-whau-au-aup, whau-au-au-au-aup" of the curlew, the croodling love-song of the peewit, and the distant call of the cuckoo in producing the May day music of the hills.

The Curlew or Whaup (Numinius arquata) is also a characteristic feature on the Dunning road as of various other glens and valleys among the Ochils, more especially of Glenquey, as already noted. Certainly the Dunning road would lack much of its charm in spring and summer if bereft of the wild, clear, tremulous whistle, dying off to the soft, wailing, quivering "wha-a-a-p" of the curlew, as he sails slowly and easily across from hill-top to hill-top, or wheels gently round, serenading his mate sitting upon her eggs on the lonely moor. The pair can also be wildly clamorous with shrill, querulous cries and angry beating of the air with their wings if we happen to approach the nest, but this we are not likely to do unless we leave the road and extend our wandering to some moorland patch away among the hills. Should we do so, there will be no difficulty in knowing when the nest is near; and unless we are simple enough to be beguiled into following the birds in their sham efforts to escape by running, we may easily find the four comparatively large handsome eggs placed quatrefoil on the primitive-looking bed of dry grass, twigs, or leaves, which is all the preparation made for their reception. They are of a pale dull green colour blotted all over with two shades of brown, and are arranged carefully in the nest with the smaller ends inwards as with those of the peewit and others of the plover tribe. They harmonise beautifully with the surrounding heather or the rough tangle of bent, tormentil, and other hill flowers. Or it may be that nothing remains in the nest but fragments of empty shell, when a further search will reveal the bonny little down-covered youngsters squatting close among the bent and heather which they very much resemble in colour – a yellowish white with spots and patches of brown. But oh! the agony of the fond parents when we take these ever so tenderly in our hands, and ugh! the deafening screams and skirls with which the old birds scold and threaten and order us to lay them down, which we are thankful to do and to get away from the ear-splitting noise.

Let us not go too far, however, till we have had a good view of the handsome birds as they alight on the ground within a few yards, in the hope of tempting us to follow them away from their darlings. The male is about 1 foot 9 inches in length, with rather long legs of a bluish colour, and a yellow bill some 6 or 7 inches in length, with a graceful curve downwards. The whole under part of a throat, breast, and body is white, more or less spotted and streaked with dark brown. The crown, back of the neck, and back, are a pale yellowish grey brown spotted with black, and the wings are brown, but most of the feathers broadly edged with white. Altogether he is a graceful and elegant bird, as well on foot as on the wing, and the opportunity of seeing him at such close quarters, and under such exciting circumstances, on his part, is well worth the trudge of a mile or so over the hill. The female is considerably larger, but does not otherwise differ much from her spouse.

Chapter Four

Academy Snapshots

The Gathering at the Unveiling Ceremony
[Photo by Mr Wm Tait (F.P.)]

70

Notes from Near and Far

UNVEILING OF WAR MEMORIAL

Dollar Magazine Vol. XX No. 79 September 1921

In our last number we gave an outline of the programme for the 28th June, when the War Memorial Monument, erected to the memory of our brave boys who "gave their all," was to be unveiled by General Davies, and we expressed the hope that there would be a large gathering of former pupils and friends. We were not disappointed. The assemblage was the largest we ever witnessed in the spacious grounds of the Academy, which, as the opening hour approached, presented a wonderful spectacle, crowds streaming towards the Memorial Monument, where seats were provided, while the pupils of all the schools formed up in the space provided for them near the platform which had been erected for the speakers and others.

Our space will not admit of anything like an adequate description of the scene. We were more impressed by it than we can say; it was one that can never be effaced from our memory, and never will be from that of anyone who witnessed it. The anthem of praise led by the School choir and orchestra; the silence during the Roll Call; the unveiling by the distinguished soldier; the Last Post by members of the Officers' Training Corps; the lament by the pipers, "The Flowers of the Forest"; and the dedicatory prayer by the parish minister – produced a grand effect, and not a heart present could remain unmoved at a scene so touching and sublime. We felt – as so many did whom we have since spoken to – filled with devotion more than by any single service we have ever heard. In fact it was unique, even in its solemnity and perfect order. An interval was granted, during which a large number of beautiful wreaths were placed at the base of the monument by relatives and friends of the fallen.

General Davies delivered an impressive address, in the course of which he said he counted it a great honour that they had asked him to come there that day to take part in that ceremony and to act on their behalf, more particularly as until that day he had never been to the School, and was unknown to most of the people connected with it. They had come together on a very great and notable occasion – such an occasion as had never before come about in the history of the famous School. They were met to do what honour they could to those men, to that woman, who had passed their childhood there, and who had given their lives in order that they who remained might live and be free. They did well to pay them honour, because they had brought to the School – an honour so great that nothing they could do could ever really repay it. He always thought that of all war memorials, perhaps the one that touched one's heart most of all was a school memorial, because one knew that these men had spent their childhood there, learned their lessons there, and played their games, and the whole place seemed haunted with their memory. He desired to say a word about the part that public schools like theirs had played, not only in this war, but in the history of the Empire. Those of them who were public school men believed (and, he thought, believed rightly) that they played a very great part indeed, and that they were a very great asset to our Empire. Wherever they went throughout the Empire they would find public school men in various posts, perhaps governing strange peoples, and always keeping up the honour and prestige of the land that bore them. He often wondered if the part that public school men had taken in the war was even now really recognised throughout the world. He once was able to bring it home to an American officer. He happened to be down at his own old school, and pointing to a long list of names in the school-yard, said: "That is our Roll of Honour." "Do you mean to tell me," said the officer, "that all these have served in this war? It is wonderful." "Served?" he said; "these are our *dead*. You will find a thousand names there if you go and count them." That officer afterwards told him that nothing he had seen or heard in this country had ever impressed him so much as the sacrifice which that school had made.

Continuing, General Davies said he wondered why it was that the public school boy bore such a part in the life of this nation. It was no answer to say that it was because he was born with a silver spoon in his mouth. The majority of them were not. The public school boy believed that it was what he learned at his school that enabled him to face the battle of life as he had done. It was what might be called the public school spirit that he learned there. It was, perhaps, most of all, what they learned outside the class-room. It was the spirit of understanding that all men are not made alike; the spirit of give and take. It was at school that they learned that essential first lesson – to obey. Having learned to obey, the public school boy, in a position of authority; in a position where words spoken by him have a great influence; in a position where he could do a great deal to make or mar the character of those younger than himself. These were the main great lessons that the public school boy took into life with him. It was a great thing to have something through life that one could hang on to. The public school boy never forgot his old school. The pride in his own school made him remember that if he did ill, it brought disgrace to his school, and if he did well, the honour and glory of his school was thereby enriched. In conclusion, General Davies said their memorial was admirably placed. The first thing that a boy would see when he came to the School would be the memorial; and it would be the last thing he would see when he went away to face the battle of life. It would give him something to live up to; and he hoped that every boy and girl who came to the School would be told at the earliest opportunity what that memorial meant, and what the people who had their names inscribed on it had done. He felt that the knowledge of what the memorial stood for would give them more than ever reason to take care that in after life they never did anything which could bring discredit to that great and noble Academy. (Applause.)

73

The hymn "For all the Saints who from their Labours Rest," was then sung, and prayer offered by Rev. P. D. Gray. The Lord's Prayer was then chanted, and the ceremony was concluded by the benediction being pronounced.

We cannot refrain from congratulating Mr Dougall, Mr McGruther, and the other members of the Staff, on the triumphant success of the proceedings of the day. Everything went off so well that it is needless to mention particulars; but the general conduct of the multitudes assembled and the contentment which so generally appeared were most gratifying.

After the unveiling ceremony a large number of the visitors sat down to luncheon in the Gymnasium of the Academy. Mr Mullan, Chairman of the Clackmannan County Education Authority, presided, and was supported on his right by General Sir Francis Davies, Major Simpson of Mawcarse, Mr R. Malcolm, and Mr Mungall, Provost of Crieff; and on his left by the Headmaster, Provost Green, Mr R. Dougall, and Mrs C. S. Dougall. The others present included:- Mr and Mrs Wm. Tait, Rev. W. B. R. Wilson, Mr Norman J. MacDonald and Mrs MacDonald, Mr Radford, Mr R. Stanhouse, Mr A. Drysdale, Captain Watson and Party, Mr Begg, Mr J. L. Sloan, Mr W. Tod Ritchie, Mr and Mrs Hodgson, Mr Jas. Campbell, Rev. J. Boyd, Mr and Mrs Allardyce, Mr MacTaggart, Mr McArthur Moir, Mrs Green, Rev. R. S. McClelland, Colonel Haig, Mr L. Bonthrone, Mr G. Bonthrone, Miss Nicolson, Mr J. B. Andrews, Mr Malcolm MacKenzie, Miss Graham, Mrs Richardson, Mr A. M. J. Graham, Mrs Macbeth, Dr and Mrs Butchart, Mr Cram, Mr, Mrs, and Master Thomas, Mr J. Patrick, Miss Dougall, Mr C. R. Dougall, Mrs Mullan, Mr J. Hogben, Mr R. Graham, Mr J.M. Cowan, Mr J. McGruther, Mr W. D. Congalton, Mr P. D. Lauder, Dr Cameron, Dr Donald Ross, Mr and Mrs Balfour, Mr and Mrs Dobie, Mr Paulin, Mr Auld, Mrs Procter, Mr J. B. Haig, Mr Brydie, Mr J. M. Ross, Mr R. W. Hepburn, Mrs Lancaster, Mrs Wallace,

Miss Wallace, Mr P. Mitchell, Mr and Mrs Wilson, Mr R. McGee, Mr T. J. Young, Mr and Mrs Morgan, Dr and Mrs Ellis, Mrs Paulin, Miss D. Robertson.

SENIOR CLASS, DOLLAR ACADEMY, SESSION 1904-05.

P. D. Lauder.

Photo.

Back Row—John F. C. Haslam. Alex. Shaw Marshall. Robert Rae M'Intosh. William Ramsay C. Callander. James Marshall.

Second Row—Andrew Whyte. Wm. D. Robieson. James M. D. Scott. Hector J. W. Hetherington. James B. Hutton.

Sitting—W. Ewart G. Munro. Robert B. Beveridge. D. Douglas Currie. David H. Whyte. Robert Bruce. John J. Turnbull. Charles Robertson.

76

Frontispiece

Dollar Magazine Vol. XIX No. 76 December 1920

We have taken as the frontispiece of this number a group of the Senior Class in Dollar Academy Session 1904-1905.

This was probably the most brilliant class ever educated in Dollar, and as such, the group is well worthy of reproduction in the *Magazine,* but its interest is, in great part, a sad one. Seventeen boys appear in the group, and two were absent on the day the photograph was taken. Of the nineteen, seven have already completed their work on earth and passed beyond the veil. We give a short note of each of them.

Robert Rae McIntosh, 2nd Lieutenant, Queen's Own Cameron Highlanders, the central figure in the back row, was killed in action on 24th April 1915. He was a distinguished student of Edinburgh University, and for a time acted as Editor of the University Magazine. Standing immediately on his left is W. Ramsay C. Callander, who graduated at St Andrews with double Honours before entering the Indian Civil Service. He was a keen sportsman, excelling in tennis and golf, and many of us remember his magnificent singing at the Boys' Concerts of his time. He died at Madras on 7th February 1918. On the extreme right of the second row is James B. Hutton, a graduate of Glasgow and Oxford. At Glasgow University he was awarded the Blackstone Gold Medal in Greek and the Ramsay Gold Medal in Latin, as well as many other distinctions. He gained the Snell Exhibition and the Newlands Scholarship, which enabled him to spend four years at Balliol College, Oxford. There he carried off the Powell Prize for Weekly Essays – a rare distinction for a Scottish student. On his return from Oxford he acted for a short time as Classical Master at Dollar. He was then appointed Lecturer in Greek Archaeology at Glasgow

University. In connection with this work, Mr Hutton was studying in Greece in the summer of this year, and to the great grief of many of his friends succumbed to fever at Smyrna on his way home.

Sitting at the left of the front row is W. Ewart G. Munro, who was killed at a level crossing on the railway near Hawthornden in December 1912. At school he earned distinction for his compositions in verse, and he followed this up by taking a foremost place in his classes at St Andrews University. From St Andrews he passed to the Edinburgh Divinity Hall of the U.F. Church, where he was the first student of his year. Sitting next to him is Robert Barrie Beveridge, also a greatly distinguished student of St Andrews. He was a medallist in all mathematical classes, and gaining a Guthrie Scholarship he proceeded to Peterhouse, Cambridge, where a brilliant career seemed to await him. During the long vacation of 1911 he was accidentally drowned while bathing off the Norfolk coast.

The absentees from the photograph are (1) David Buchan, Lieutenant, Gordon Highlanders, killed in action in April 1917, who was also a distinguished student of St Andrews, and gave great promise of becoming a notable minister of the U.F. Church of Scotland; and (2) Matthew W. Robieson, one of the most brilliant scholars Dollar has ever produced. In Glasgow University he won every philosophical distinction open to him, as well as the Logan Gold Medal awarded to the most distinguished Graduate in Arts in Glasgow. He also gained the Ferguson Scholarship, open to all four Scottish Universities. After serving for a period as Assistant to Sir Henry Jones in the Moral Philosophy Department of Glasgow, he was appointed Lecturer in Moral Philosophy in the Queen's University, Belfast. There he did work which will prove of permanent value, and was rapidly coming to the forefront of his profession when he was drowned while bathing at St Mervyn, Cornwall, on the 16th July 1919. His twin brother, William D.

Robieson, is second from the left in the middle row. The brothers went together to Glasgow, after sharing the Wilson Memorial Prize Bursary list, and soon established themselves in a high place among the students of the day. William specialised in History, and was for a time assistant to the Professor of the subject in Glasgow. After research work in Italy, and for a period of service as a soldier, he joined the staff of the *Glasgow Herald*, a position which he still holds. On his left is James Duncan Scott, a former Milne Medallist, and now a distinguished member of the medical profession. Next to him is Hector J. W. Hetherington, also a former Milne Medallist, now Principal of Exeter University College. Like Matthew Robieson, he gained every philosophical distinction open to him in Glasgow, as well as the Ferguson Scholarship. He acted for some time as assistant to Sir Henry Jones, and later was appointed Professor of Moral Philosophy in University College, Cardiff.

The names of all in the group appear below the print of the photograph. All are worthy of honourable mention, as may be instanced by the bare statement that Captain Haslam, R. A. M. C., standing on the left of the back row, and Captain Robertson, Gordon Highlanders, sitting on the right of the front row, were both awarded the Military Cross.

Only lack of space prevents us from going over the record of each in detail. We know that we are speaking for all the Dollar teachers who had the privilege of instructing this class, when we say that we are proud of their record, and we venture to hold it up as an example and incentive to the pupils of to-day.

Chapter Five

Local History

Photo by A. P. Russell.

THE OLD TOWN, FROM THE GOLF COURSE.

82

"An Appearance", a Disappearance, and a Snap-Shot

By T J Alfred Scott

Dollar Magazine Vol. 1 No. 1 – March 1902

This is a true story without embellishment or literary pretension. It is better that this should be understood at the outset. Although the scythe of Time has made sad havoc with the years since its occurrence, there are fortunately men alive to-day who can confirm its every detail, and who will, I am sure (as a personal favour), acquit me of exaggeration. Indeed, were it not for this comforting knowledge, I would hesitate to open the book of memory at so uncanny a page.

Beyond these necessary words, I attempt no preface. The facts must speak for themselves. In the end Truth usually prevails, as you will find it emphatically does in this case.

A great fear had fallen upon Dollar – not all at once, but by a series of spasms, even many of the more staid and orthodox members of the community finally becoming victims to the impalpable dread. First one, then another, then a score gave their testimony, and it was generally a whispered and trembling one. Although differing at times in what, doubtless, were important details, there was invariably a wonderful unanimity of agreement in the main points of their experience. Common-sense (in the daylight) fought valiantly for the victory; but when the November mists swathed the hills – creeping stealthily down to the village through the weirdness of the glen, its rout was complete, and the bravest of us was demoralised. A ghost had taken possession of the old churchyard!

Pardon the brusque announcement. I had hoped to approach the climax cautiously and with discretion; but try as I would, there was no holding *it* back. Playing leap-frog over the intervening years, as it did long ago over the tombstones, the memory of the awful Shape has sprung upon me as I write.

I have always understood that it was a very small boy who first discovered the ghost, and that in running home (to tell his mother) he threw a stone at it. Be this as it may, very soon a jolly-faced Rumour, with a knowing wink, trotted about disseminating the "joke"; and, as a consequence, the following night, a miscellaneous deputation of all ages (clinging very closely together, for the weather was cold), crossed the bridge to interview the newcomer; but just within sight of the old kirk ruins, they hurriedly separated to fulfil pressing engagements elsewhere.

Little by little the fearsome story was spun together, and a gruesome pattern it made. In the telling of it (and I am afraid in the listening too), hair stood on end that had always been modest and unassertive before, while unfamiliar shivers titillated the bald pates of elderly gentlemen, whose courage, so far, had never been called in question. And the erstwhile jocund Rumour was lachrymose and sad, pacing the streets like a one-man funeral.

Reader, have you ever seen a ghost? I put the question in all seriousness, for, on such a subject, it would ill become me to be flippant. There was a man once, who on being asked if he knew German, replied in the negative; but (being a self-respecting individual) he consoled himself by adding that he had a cousin who played the German concertina. This was, I suppose, as near as he could conscientiously get to it. You may have met people whose knowledge of ghosts is on somewhat similar lines. They are willing to admit, in a vague sort of way – indeed they are rather proud of it – that far back in the "misty past" (subsequent to the dynasty of

84

Adam, of course) there was a tradition in their family of ---; you know the usual style of these legends, and can fill in the hiatus for yourselves. For my part, I am no cynic. I recognise the value of ghosts – and gout – as ancestral adjuncts. Yet, suggestive though they are of such aristocratic items as turret chambers and crusted port, a *personal* acquaintance with either is not desirable; and I, for one, would prefer to leave them to the genial hospitality of, say, the Norman era. But, unfortunately, I commenced by saying that this is a veritable statement of facts; so even at the risk of being laughed at, I feel bound to relate my own experience.

Yet I cannot help lingering on the threshold. Life is full of ghosts. Dead years, like the withered leaves of a long-ago autumn, litter the travelled road; and old familiar faces haunt its every turn and corner. But it is good to know that most of these greet us with a smile of welcome. Since the early Dollar days, my lot has been cast in many strange lands, yet there is hardly an inch of the bonnie valley that I cannot people with old associations. Boy faces, merry voices, and school-time happenings are among the flowers of memory. And this will be your experience by-and-by – those of you who are lads and lasses now. When you are weary in the journey of life – which may happen often – your hearts will go out to the old school playground, where you were so active once – and rest there; or to the hills, where the sheep will seem the identical sheep of your boyhood. For myself I can truthfully say, that in all my wanderings I never thought of "mutton" in their connection; and while I look into their patient faces to-day, I am – for the time being – a vegetarian. Is it a wonder, then, that on my return, I knew them, every one – or fancied I did – it matters not which? Out upon the vandal, say I, who would add mint sauce to the "little lamb" which we have known from childhood, "Mary had ---!" Don't smile, this is a utilitarian age, an age that sneers at sentiment, and, with brazen effrontery, affects to disbelieve in ghosts!

Luckily, however, for my credit's sake, what *I* saw was no trick of an irresponsible imagination; but, as the sequel will show, had an actual and tangible existence. Although I was only a boy at the time, I shall never forget that terrible night.

Ten o'clock struck as I sneaked out of the house on my lonely adventure. It was a fine, still night, and the streets were dark and deserted, when at last I reached the precincts of the old kirkyard. A gentle ripple of air whispered among the trees, awakening responsive murmurings from their partially denuded branches. The great expanse of sky pulsated with stars: little delicate clouds drifting lazily over the moon, and throwing faint uneven shadows on the grass. No sound, save the indistinct chatter of the burn, broke the "monotony of silence." The toils of an undefinable expectancy seemed to hold me prisoner; and I shuddered involuntarily as I peered through the bars of the iron gate.

Then *it* came – moving noiselessly among the shadows, and eerily creeping in and out among the head-stones, with wing-like arms outstretched – a tall, grey *Thing!* My first glimpse of the dread appearance was as it glided, with a sinuous waving motion, from the leafage of ivy, which, at that time, clothed the ruined walls of that ancient church. I dared not stir, I hardly dared to breathe. For a time my heart seemed to stop its beating as I watched; then, all at once, in an uncontrollable paroxysm of fear, it burst into wild throbbings, for, to my horror, the awesome figure, with a sudden swirl of its extended arms, turned as if to approach my hiding-place!

I remember little else; but even to-day I can hear the clatter of my feet as I leapt down the brae and over the bridge, never stopping in my wild race until I reached home, panting and exhausted, crying out, "I've seen the ghost; I've seen the ghost!"

But, fortunately for the mental equilibrium of the village – and mine in particular – a Nemesis was on the track of that spectre. A Psychical Research Society had been hastily inaugurated, under the presidency of one of Dr Lindsay's older boarders, and it soon got to work. Marching to the gate in a body, a night or two after my encounter, the corporate and official optic of the association speedily focussed the unwelcome visitor, whose genuflections were much the same as when it had appeared to me. But the president was not daunted. Pulling an old pistol from his pocket, and pointing it with a more or less steady hand at the intruder, he sternly demanded instant surrender. "Mind, I'll shoot," said he; and, after a pause, he slowly counted "One – two – three – !" No answer. Then – *snap* went the trigger! A great yell, which sent a chill to the hearts of the listeners, and scared the sleeping birds from the ivy, echoed through the night, as the poor bedraggled "apparition" rushed towards the gate. "Dinna shoot, dinna shoot! it's only me; it's only Dawvid!" And, sure enough it *was* "Muckle Dawvid" of the Gas Works, cleverly enveloped in an enormous sheet, which, however, in his terror, had partially detached itself from his shoulders, and was floating behind him like a storm-sped cloud.

Next morning every one had heard the news. It ran like wildfire through the village, and a combined sigh of relief went up gratefully to the heavens. Our old friend, the jolly-faced Rumour, was once more in great demand, after his temporary overthrow. All day he was busy ladling out the details, variously seasoned to suit each variety of palate; and you know how much that sort of delicacy is appreciated, even in these later days. Why "Dawvid" had acted so foolishly, no one could tell, and *he* was mute on the subject. True, it was suggested by some, that long working among gas might have made him *light*-headed. But when it was remembered that the libelled illuminant was *Dollar* gas, no one believed it.

This sketch is already too long, or it would be instructive to recount some of the artful dodges whereby the "fathers" sought to set themselves right in their own and each other's estimation; for when the evening shadows lay in the lap of the hills, a little crowd gathered on the brig to discuss matters. I must content myself, however, by simply placing on record the fact that amid much smoking, some sly nudges, and not a few suggestive winks, it was ultimately decided, by common consent, that each of them was entitled to return to the bosom of an admiring family, with bonnet cocked as of yore, completely absolved from even the suspicion of a belief in "gaists, wraiths, or similar devilish superstitions."

But it seemed to me that the listening burn, footing it over the stones under the brig after its journeyings among the mysteries of the glen, chuckled and laughed as though it knew better and thoroughly enjoyed the joke.

An Ochil Tragedy

By G L

Dollar Magazine Vol. II No. 5 – March 1903

Thomas Dalgleish, a native of Dollar, aged twenty-two years, and George Campbell, a boy of fifteen, belonging to Tillicoultry, left the latter place on a Sunday morning in January 1850 with the view of visiting some friends in Blackford, and returning the same afternoon. Favoured with a bright, crisp day, they safely reached their destination, and about three o'clock in the afternoon made preparations for the return journey. Now, however, the sun had got eclipsed, and the heavens were assuming a threatening aspect, and the young lad, who had scarcely recovered from the fatigue of crossing, and dreading a storm, pled with the older and stronger youth to remain until the next morning. On the other hand, Dalgleish, who knew the hills well, and was anxious to get home that night, in order to be in time for the sport of next day (Handsel Monday), would neither listen to the advice of his friends nor the entreaties of the boy, and eventually both set out on a journey which proved painfully disastrous and tragic. In a short time after they left the sky began to lower, the wind howled and roared, and a snowstorm set in, which raged with fury all through a moonless, starless night, and the greater part of the next day. This sudden and severe storm was the cause of painful anxiety to the relations of the two youths, who, for aught that they knew, might be struggling and battling against it, with no human help at hand, but they endeavoured to console themselves with the hope that their friends in Blackford, seeing the threatening aspect of the weather, would have induced them not to risk such a perilous journey.

When Handsel Monday night came, without any tidings of their whereabouts, the relatives entertained the gravest fears of their safety, and it was now resolved to send messengers at break of day round both by Dunblane and Glendevon to Blackford, to see what light could be thrown on the movements of the hapless youths. On arriving at that place, having heard nothing of them on the way, and learning that they had set out to cross the hills on Sunday afternoon, and further, that they had not been seen nor heard of at the Backhills house, all hope of their safety vanished, as it was almost impossible that any human being could have survived that awful night without aid or shelter.

All along the Hillfoots the keenest interest was evinced in the fate of these young lads. Money was raised and search parties were organised to scour the hills along the line of route generally taken in crossing; but as the frost was intense, the snow deep, and in many places drifted into immense wreaths, the task was fatiguing and not a little hazardous. On three different days this melancholy work was willingly engaged in, and on the last of these the body of the poor boy was found deeply embedded in the snow, head downmost, in a part of Maddy Moss, not far from the beaten track. Meanwhile it was deemed advisable to delay further search for the young man until the snow was reduced in depth, as it was suspected he lay deeply buried in it. Towards the end of February it was resolved to make another grand effort to recover the body of Dalgleish, and hundreds of young men from Dollar, Tillicoultry, and Alva willingly offered their services. It was arranged that search parties should leave each of these towns early on Sunday morning (exactly six weeks after the tragic event happened), and scour the glens leading to Alva Moss and Maddy Moss, and finally concentrate about the head of Tillicoultry Glen. I remember being roused out of sleep early that Sunday morning by the blowing of horns and the sound of many voices, which turned out to be a large contingent sent from

Tillicoultry to strengthen and accompany the one from Dollar, which was to proceed up by Castle Campbell.

There are some sights which, seen in boyhood, are never effaced from the memory, and what I saw that afternoon is still vividly before me. About five o'clock, on coming out of the Sunday School, which was then held in the Original Secession Church (now Mayfield), and reaching the Burnside, we saw a cart turning the corner of the street immediately behind, and proceeding towards the Old Town. On making up to it we were startled and awestruck to find that lying on a bed of straw and rolled in a shepherd's plaid was the corpse of Dalgleish, stiff and rigid, the feet exposed and projecting beyond the cart, the back door of which having been removed, and like children, we followed with almost breathless curiosity mingled with solemnity this rustic and melancholy cortege, until it reached the house of his grandmother with whom he had always lived.

That forenoon one of the contingent which had been searching the hills to the west of Bencleuch discovered the body of Dalgleish deeply embedded in snow, nothing being seen but part of his coat sticking through, and miles away from the ordinary track generally taken when crossing either from Dollar or Tillicoultry.

Judging from where he was found, the boy Campbell, by reason of his tender years and the effect of his exertions that forenoon – thus little fitted to bear the strain of a violent snowstorm, especially on the pathless hills – perished early in the evening. Doubtless Dalgleish, who must have keenly felt his responsibility in this trying situation, strained every nerve to save the life of his companion, but whether they got accidentally separated during that blinding storm – in which case the boy must have succumbed quickly and quietly – or whether the young man suffered the cruel agony of witnessing the death of his comrade, and then made a desperate dash for dear life,

91

will never be known. Beyond all doubt Dalgleish, who was both daring and powerfully built, must have struggled for life like a very hero during the greater part of that night. This is evident when it is considered that his body was found several miles to the west of the direct road either to Tillicoultry or Dollar and across a region wind-swept and rough even in fine weather.

Had he not lost his way – having turned west instead of east – he seems to have had strength enough and gone far enough to have landed him within sight of his own home; but mist and snow-drift, especially in the wide expanse of a pathless, hilly region, all the more so when darkness has set in, is confusing and bewildering, and now and again even proves fatal to shepherds who are otherwise quite at home in these wild solitudes.

The Drysdales of Dollar

By the Rev. Robert Paul, F.S.A.Scot.

Dollar Magazine Vol. VIII No. 29 – March 1909

We are all, I suppose, familiar with the fact that certain surnames abound in various parts of our country, and have continued to do so for a very long period. Notable illustrations are to be found in the case of the Highland clans, such as the Campbells in Argyll, the Grants in Strathspey, the Camerons in Lochaber and Lochiel, and the Mackays in Sutherland. And the same applies to the Border septs, like the Johnstones of Annandale, the Armstrongs and Elliots of Liddesdale, and the Homes of the Merse. In all these localities the patronymics borne by the families originally possessing, or at all events inhabiting, the lands and acknowledging a common ancestry, still largely prevail. It may be said, indeed, that almost every part of Scotland has surnames, peculiar to itself, and still prevailing there more largely than elsewhere, notwithstanding the migratory and shifting habits of modern days. Along the "Hillfoots," for example, such names as Kirk, Alexander, Burns, Dawson, Glass, Harley, and others that might be mentioned are of frequent occurrence to-day, and they can all be traced back as existing in the locality for a very long time – in the case of some of them even hundreds of years.

Amongst these one of the most notable is that of Drysdale. This cognomen is frequently met with at the present day in the west of Fife, and more or less throughout what was known in ancient times as the territory of Fothrik, Forthriffe, or Forthreve, the part of the country which may be described generally as that between Loch Leven and Stirling from east to west, and between the Ochils and the Forth from north to south. And the popular belief in the district is that the name first came into use in our own parish of Dollar, and under circumstances detailed in the following interesting and curious document, which is said to have been preserved among the various representatives of the family in this district for many generations:–

"On the twentieth day of May, one thousand five hundred and three years, we, Thomas, William, and James Douglas, sons of the departed Thomas Douglas of Brushwood Haugh in the parish of Drysdale and shire of Dumfries, left our native place for the reason here assigned, viz, defending our just and lawful rights against our unjust neighbour, Johnston of Greenstonehill, who, being determined to bring water to his mill through our property, and having obtained leave of his friend, the King, began his operations on Monday, the 16th May. We prevented him by force. The next day he brought twenty of his vassals to carry on the work. We, with two friends and three servants (eight in all), attacked Johnston with his twenty, and in the contest fourteen of his men were killed along with their base leader. A report of these proceedings was carried to the King, and we were obliged to fly (the tocsin[1] being sounded). We took shelter under the shadow of the Ochil Hills, in a lonely valley on the river Devon. After having lived there full two years, we returned home in disguise, but found all our property in possession of Johnston's friends, and a great reward offered for our lives. We, having purchased a small spot, called the Haugh of Dollar, and changed our names to the name of our native parish, were clearly in mind to spend the residue of our days under the ope of the Ochils, and wish the name of Drysdale to flourish in the lonely valley. The King passed through this with his court on the 12th of June 1506, going from Stirling to Falkland; dined on Haliday's green (an eastern neighbour); but we were not recognised."

---

[1] The alarm bell

There seems no reason to doubt the credibility of the story thus recorded, whatever may be said of the authenticity of the document itself. For at the period mentioned the Borderland was in a most disorganised state, and conflicts between the turbulent Border clans – of whom the Douglases and the Johnstons were amongst the most prominent – were of constant occurrence. Nor were these members of the former tribe who are said to have fled from their native Dryfesdale to the northern shire of Clackmannan by any means singular or alone in so doing, or in their change of name with a view to secure immunity for their violence. For it is on record that some forty years before this time – in 1460 – two younger sons of Sir Adam Johnstone of Westerraw in the Upper Ward of Lanarkshire, scions of the very family with whom the Douglases of Brushwood Haugh were at deadly variance, fled from their native district in consequence of "some discontent," and settled in Perthshire, assuming "to themsellfs the sirname of Souter, that therby they should not be noticed for the tyme."[2] "One of the breathers dyeing without issue, the other surviveing, for his good deportment was married to a gentlewoman, from which marriage proceedit diverse honest men." These "honest men," with their families, who, it is mentioned, were "considerable," bore the name of Souter for upwards of a century, when, by Act of the Scottish Parliament, 21st August 1663, in the reign of Charles II, they were permitted to resume their true and ancient surname of Johnstone, the Act declaring that "this change shall nowayes prejudge them nor their airs and successors."

It is further evidence of the credibility of this story that as a tradition it has been long known in the locality where the incidents referred to in it are said to have occurred, and that many attempts have been made in the past to identify the exact location of Brushwood Haugh

---

[2] "Genealogy and Surnames," by William Anderson, Edinburgh, 1865, p. 114.

and Greenstonehill, but unfortunately without success. I have recently made extensive researches in every available source of documentary authority, and also in the district, without being able definitely to locate them. The names have utterly disappeared, and are quite unknown even to natives quite familiar with its topography and history.

The parish of Dryfesdale, popularly pronounced Drysdale, is situated in the centre of Annandale in the south of Dumfriesshire, and takes its name from the Water of Dryfe which flows through it in a south-westerly direction to join the river Annan. Along the banks of the stream are wide tracts of rich holm land, the depositions of the water from time immemorial, consisting of deep loam, easy of culture, and luxuriantly fertile.[3] Before joining the Annan, and after traversing the parish for some two and a half miles, the deposits which it makes, and the stretch of level land which it occasionally desolates with its floods, is called Dryfe Sands. This place is memorable as the scene of a sanguinary conflict between the Maxwells and the Johnstones, in which the former, though much superior in numbers, were vanquished and pursued, and lost on the field and in the retreat seven hundred men, including Lord Maxwell, their commander, many of the wounded, it is said, being cut down in the streets of the neighbouring town of Lockerbie.

From a courteous correspondent in that town,[4] I have received information which makes it tolerably certain that the sites of Brushwood Haugh and Greenstonehill were somewhere on the banks of the Dryfe in the holm-land in the northern part of the parish. This information was communicated by a Mr Kerr, a native

---

[3] The Dryfe's impetuosity and its property of "driving" all before it at times is supposed to be the origin of its name.

[4] Mr Thomas Henderson, solicitor, to whom my best thanks are due for the amount of trouble he has taken on my behalf.

of the locality and an official of the Caledonian Railway Company, now resident at Carstairs, whose opinion is that they were at or near a spot called Old Walls in the Dryfe Valley. This place is still a farm about two and a quarter miles north of Lockerbie, and a mile above Lockerbie House, which before 1881 had long been the home of a family of Johnstones, and later of the Johnstone-Douglases of Lockerbie. Old Walls lies on the east side of the river Dryfe, and about a mile farther up on the other side is Lammonbie Mill. Mr Kerr's great-great-great-grandfather was tenant of Lammonbie Farm and his great-grandfather was tenant of the farm of Lockerbie Hill. His grandfather, who was born in 1777, was for fifty years baron officer here to Mr Johnstone-Douglas of Lockerbie, and Mr Kerr says that he had frequently heard the story of the Drysdales from his grandfather, who always affirmed that the scene of the dispute was in the vicinity of what is now Lammonbie Mill, and that the places named, or at least one of them, were situated near Old Walls. This is the more probable as the lower end of Dryfe Water has long been the home of the Johnstones, and the locus is one of the few places in the parish suitable for a mill, or indeed possible for one to be.

The wish expressed by the Douglas refugees that the name they had assumed might flourish "in the lonely valley on the River Devon," was abundantly fulfilled. For in the course of the century following their settlement there, their descendants are found located as portioners, feuars, and tenants in different parts of the parish and surrounding districts. In 1536 a William Draisdale was bailiff at Alva to Sir William Monteith of West Kerse, who was then the proprietor of that estate, and another member of the family, and of the same Christian name, was chief officer of the garrison of Lochleven Castle under Sir William Douglas of 1567, and was one of the most wary and relentless jailers of the unfortunate Queen

Mary, during her confinement there.[5] A "Sir Andro Drisdell" occurs in a minute of the Regality Court of the Barony of Alloa, dated 20th June 1554. From the Register of Dunfermline Abbey it appears that about 1557 a tack of "three bovates of the Mains of Dollar" was granted by the monastery there to an Agnes Dryisdaill and her husband Andrew Vannand. Four of the name, a Thomas, a William and two Johns – one of the latter being designated "alias Gregoursone" – were among the original feuars of the Dollar lands belonging to the Regality of Campbell, when these were first feued by the Earl of Argyll in 1605. In 1620 Simon Drysdale, one of their immediate descendants, was still in possession of the Haugh of Dollar, the original settlement of the fugitives from Dumfries-shire. And in the Commissariot Record of Stirling, the wills of twenty-seven persons of the name in the parish of Dollar, evidently persons of substance more or less, are registered between 1615 and 1685.

The reference at the end of the above document to the passing of the king (James IV) and his court on their way from Stirling to Falkland in June 1506 is interesting, because in connection with it there is still current in Kinross-shire a curious tradition as to an incident in the royal progress which is said to have occurred on this occasion at Tullibole Castle near the Crook of Devon, and the memory of which is still preserved by a local designation. The king and his retinue were hospitably entertained in passing by the laird of Tullibole, and the tables were erected in a field in the neighbourhood of the Castle – the "Haliday's green" of the document. Among the king's attendants was a trooper celebrated for his bacchanalian prowess, and among the vassals of the laird there was one named Keltie equally renowned for the same questionable pre-eminence. The two

---

[5] Burns-Begg's "History of Lochleven," in 1887, where a full account is given of the stratagem by means of which the captive queen endeavoured, but unsuccessfully, to provide for Drysdale's absence from the castle on the day of her escape.

challenged each other to a drinking bout, but having no opportunity of pitting their powers against one another while the king was present, they agreed to meet on the following morning on the same spot where his majesty had dined. It is not said what kind of liquor they drank, but they drank it out of a "quaff" as it was called – a small wooden vessel holding about half an English pint. They continued to drink for three days, when the trooper fell from his seat apparently asleep. Keltie thereupon took another draught to show that he was conqueror, and this gave rise to a proverb in the district "Keltie's Mends." It was customary thereafter when any person refused to drink off his glass that he was threatened with "Keltie's Mends." Keltie, it is said, afterwards dropped also from his seat and fell asleep, but when he awoke he found his companion dead. He was buried where he lay, and as the place was near a small pool of water, it still retains the name of "the Trooper's Dub." The ghost of the unfortunate trooper was believed to haunt the spot, and the Rev. Mr Graham, the writer of the Old Statistical Account of the parish, says that in his day (1776) few of the country people cared to pass the Trooper's Dub at night.

The "Haliday's Green" of the above document, however, militates strongly against its authenticity as an account contemporary with the incidents it purports to relate; for, as may be learned from the article on Tullibole Castle in the present number of the *Dollar Magazine,* the proprietor in 1506 was Andrew Hering of Glasclune, and the Hallidays did not come into possession of it until a century later. This indeed seems to me to be conclusive proof that the old Drysdale manuscript printed above is not really a production of the sixteenth century, as it professes to be, but must be relegated to a much later date. It is possible that the story was perpetuated orally among the Drysdales till the following century, when it was committed to writing, and was composed in the first person to give it greater verisimilitude. In several copies of it which I have seen, a note is appended to the effect that it was copied first by Simon

Drysdale of the Haugh of Dollar in the year 1620, as well as by subsequent representatives of the family. Probably "first copied" should be "first committed to writing." The story itself, however, as I have already said, is not at all improbable. It may be added that though it professes to give the origin of the branch of the Drysdales in our part of the country, the name was already known elsewhere, and is found occurring even in this same district some twenty-seven years before. For in one of the burgh records of Stirling it is recorded that on the 16th May 1478, a Thomas Drusdale – who was evidently an ecclesiastic, from the "Dominus" (the Latin equivalent of our "Sir," usually at this period applied to certain priests) prefixed to his name – appeared before the Abbot and Convent of Cambuskenneth about his lease of Alveth (Alva) Church. And the same Thomas Drysdale appears as a witness to a sasine of James Shaw of Salchy (Sauchie), of the five merk land of Tullibody, dated 11th March 1478. But in those times ecclesiastics were a wandering folk, and his presence in the Hillfoots was probably a mere sporadic or solitary occurrence.

The Rough Bounds of Knoydart with Billy

("A fine quiet pony")

Dollar Magazine – February 1954

There was a time once when the three men thought nothing of packing the bare necessities of life into a rucksack and setting off into the blue to walk great distances, climb high mountains, and stay away as long as possible from the noise, rush, and turmoil of present-day life.

With the passing of years these expeditions became shorter and the boasting of the three men greater. Long walks and climbs were talked about, but nothing was done until one day the daddy of the three had a brilliant idea – a pony to carry not just the necessities of life but also some of the comforts.

What a picture came to mind of blue skies, rushing burns, high mountains, lonely lochs to fish, and the pleasure of wandering over hill tracks with nothing to carry, far from the beaten track, at peace with the world.

Truly that faithful, sure-footed, clever friend of man, the Highland garron, would make our holiday. But where to find one? The Highland factor is a man with strange ideas of those who roam the hills and is inclined to classify all the fresh air fraternity as "hikers." We were advised strongly to join a pony school at Kingussie where, with thirty others, we might take daily excursions to the foot of the mountains and return each evening to the comforts of an excellent hotel.

This, however, did not fit in with our ideas, and great credit was given to the man responsible for the scheme, for not only did he find a pony whose owner was willing to hire, but found it at no great distance from the proposed starting place. With his previous knowledge of horses and the assurance from the owner that the beast was sound in wind and limb and free from vice, our holiday became a certainty.

The route was to be from Strathan at the head of Loch Arkaig, through Glen Dessarry to Sourlies on Loch Nevis, up the River Carnach, and west by Glen Meadail to the Inverie River. Then north-east to Barrisdale Bay on Loch Hourn and east along that loch to Kinlochourn, thence to Loch Quoich, and so from there via Glen Kingie back to Strathan. The expedition was to be led by the man who had arranged the pony; secretary, treasurer, and official photographer was the banker; the third man – responsible for catering and equipment – the cook.

Everything was worked out in great detail, wives were called in for consultation, balanced diets and vitamins discussed, the pony insured, and we were scarcely ready when the great day at last arrived. These were the plans, but the best laid schemes gang aft agley.

One glorious morning in early June we left the sleeping city behind and headed north. Blair Atholl was the first stop where the deer saddle was picked up; it was very heavy and completely filled the back of our two-seater. We wondered what the garron would think of it and how all our varied bits and pieces hung from it would compare with a dead stag; one thing was certain, the weight would not be so great.

Once past Struan the holiday really started. We sang about Bonny Prince Charlie, the West, the Hebrides, and even got the length of

"Galway Bay." Lunch was taken beside a rushing stream near Dalwhinnie, and that usually rather bleak spot was beautiful in sunshine. Later, the Loch Laggan hills stood out bold and clear, then, past Spean Bridge, the mighty Ben Nevis came into view, cloudless, and with only one tiny spot of snow high up on the cliffs. There had been a long dry spell in the west; surely it would last another week.

The road from Achnarry runs along Loch Arkaig. The scenery is magnificent and the road surface easily the worst in Scotland. These 14 miles seemed to take ages, but at long last the car bounced round a corner and there was the shepherd's house, the single-room tin school, and a cattle float.

The garron's master and the driver of the float, with his small son, sat admiring the view and keeping the midges at bay. They were anxious to be on their way, so Billy was introduced at once. "A fine quiet beast," said the owner. "Indeed he is a fine quiet beast," said the driver and, as Billy cropped the grass contentedly, that appeared to be a fair description. He paid not the slightest attention to his master's farewell as the float bounced and bumped out of sight. A sheep fank and old shed, surrounded by a high fence, was very handy for our first night; the tent was erected with a view of those shapely mountains, Streap and Sgor nan Coireachan, towering above Glen Pean. Then the arranging of stores began in the shed. It was necessary to have the weight evenly distributed on each side of the saddle and we had four shaped waterproof bags for this purpose. Everything was laid out in order and it really looked as if we had twice as much as any normal garron could carry; but Billy was no ordinary beast, as we were later to learn. He came into the shed to see what was going on and promptly started to eat a loaf of bread. Our pony man had no easy job persuading him to stay out.

103

Late that evening the party was completed by the arrival of the banker, who promptly gave a lurid description of the Loch Arkaig road in very strong language. He was right away promoted assistant pony man, as the leader felt certain Billy would understand such language.

Next morning mist was well down on the hills, and, as we packed, a fine rain started. It became quite heavy as the saddle was placed in position and the bags arranged on each side. On top were the small tent, cooking utensils, Billy's oats, and the etceteras. It looked a considerable load, but there was still a lot left for the three men to carry. Looking very coy in a lady's waterproof hat and extra long fisherman's oilskin, the leader set off leading Billy; cook and banker followed to pick up what might fall off the swaying load. It looked somewhat like a Biblical picture.

The pass from Strathan through Glen Dessarry to the head of Loch Nevis is about 12 miles over Mam na Cloich Airde; it rises from 100 to 1,000 ft., then drops to sea level. In the days of long ago cattle were driven through regularly, and how those drovers managed was quite beyond our understanding after we had completed the journey.

Going west it was a pleasant walk to the summit, but there we struck very wet bog. In pouring rain and a cold west wind we tried to pick a way over firm ground, and were progressing very slowly when Billy suddenly got bogged right up to his houghs. It looked as if the load would have to come off, and very quickly, when Billy, with the most tremendous effort and sounds of loud squelching, shot out, knocked the pony man over, and stood looking down with disdain at our poor, wet, and muddy leader.

After we had struggled over some very nasty rocks, where Billy again distinguished himself by negotiating a 3-ft drop, the track appeared again and was more or less level for a mile, but to our dismay it now climbed sharply in a series of steep zigzags. This ascent took a long time, then worse was to follow, for below was a most horrible-looking descent which to us appeared impossible for any laden animal. Part of the load was taken off and carried down the hill, but this proved to be unnecessary. Billy very cleverly picked his way down the steepest and most slippery slopes without any trouble and eventually we emerged from the mist, and there before us was Loch Nevis.

It was now 7 p.m. and we had been walking since 10 a.m. with very little food or rest. There was a half-ruined house at the head of Loch Nevis and our one thought was shelter and a meal.

Troubles seemed at an end and it was a great relief to walk without going up and down. Then the blow came. A normally small stream crossing the track had become a raging torrent, about 4 ft. deep, with large, round stones on the bottom. We stood in the pouring rain, four very cold dejected figures, three thinking of a nightmare journey back over the track. Then the banker, without a word, plunged in and got across, soaked well above the waist. The cook was handed the halter and followed, leaving the pony man to do his best in the rear. Billy was our problem, but we need not have worried. Carefully he picked his way across, then charged up the steep rise on the opposite side, knocking banker and cook over on his way to the top, where he waited patiently for the party to join him. The half-ruined house now came into view and even in its dilapidated condition was a sight for tired eyes. (This place is called Sourlies and here for many years lived a charming old couple, Mr and Mrs John McPherson. There is, of course, no road, and the nearest town is Mallaig, from which twice a week, weather permitting, chugs a motor boat with mail and the necessities of life. When John died some years ago, Mrs McPherson, who had no means of getting in touch with anyone, built a bonfire and made a smoke screen which eventually was seen and brought help. The pony man had stayed there when old John was alive and in the course of conversation had asked: "Don't you find it very lonely here sometimes?" "No, no," said Mrs McPherson, "there is always something happening. If the tide is not coming in, it is going out!")

That evening there was a great deal happening. Billy had his oats in the stable, which was in better condition than the house, and had plenty of hay to lie on, or munch, as he wished. The three men managed to get a fire going and had a very large meal and large nightcap, and so to bed in rather damp sleeping bags to sleep as if on spring mattresses.

Next day was fine and warm, and how pleasant it was after the previous day's experience to wander down the shore of Loch Nevis, admiring the view of endless mountains, blue loch, and blue sky. Billy was completely draped with drying clothes, only his face showing, but he appeared quite happy and stopped very frequently to munch some extra tasty grass. About one and a half miles down the loch we turned north and followed the Carnach River. Here the floor of the valley was a mass of sea pinks. Sgor na Ciche, one of the shapeliest of all mountains, towered in front of us and the river was our only obstacle. However, to-day was different – it was warm. We stripped and Billy made no objection to the crossing.

All too soon the track started to climb in steep zigzags, but we stopped often and lay in the sunshine while Billy cropped peacefully. At this point the sole of the pony man's shoe came off. This was serious and he was at once demoted. Cook was given the halter and proudly he started off with his new charge. The garron had his own ideas of climbing: for about fifty paces he went hard, pushing you hard in the back if you lagged, then suddenly he would stop and nothing would persuade him to move till he was ready.

The shoe, or the warm sunshine, or the exquisite view caused much delay with the rearguard, and cook found himself very much alone high up the mountain with an animal he was not very sure of. Here the only sign of life was an eagle, wheeling majestically high above the rocky tops. The silence at each stop was complete, the scenery rather awe-inspiring, and the drop at some parts of the narrow track considerable. Cook realised he knew more about primus stoves and frying pans than garrons, and felt a bit nervous.

From here the track could be seen descending in an easy gradient and ere long we were down, forded the River Meadail, and after a pleasant walk through the first trees we had seen for some time, came to a narrow bridge. Near it was a large herd of Highland cattle, from very small calves to a ferocious-looking bull. They were most interested and we thought it best not to linger, but Billy did not like the bridge. We spoke nicely to him, coaxed him, took his load off, promised him double rations, but he stuck his forelegs out and would not budge. Boilings were no use, and then the pony man remembered bread. Billy could not resist and over he clattered for his loaf. At the other side of the river was the most delightful camping spot. Soon the tent up, Billy fed, and the evening meal cooking.

During dinner our four-legged friend managed to get his hind legs tied up with the tether rope every few minutes. It became a bit monotonous undoing this so Billy was then securely tied to a tree, and we had almost finished the meal in peace when there was the sound of hoofs on the bridge.

"It is alright," said the pony man, "there is a gate at the other side;" but cook went to find out the cause of the bother. Approaching the bridge, he saw Billy back off stern first, kick his heels in the air, and set off upstream.

Here the river took a wide curve, so it seemed easy to head Billy back to camp. We raced across and closed in on him but landed in very boggy ground. Billy on the bank turned round and appeared to laugh, then plunged in, swam across, again kicked up his back legs, neighed loudly, and set off at full speed for home, followed by the herd of Highland cattle. The last we saw of Billy was the pony high up on the track we had descended that afternoon. When he took his first rest he turned round and, looking towards us, no doubt said in horse language, "You've had it, chums."

The night was cold, spirits a bit low, and another large nightcap necessary. No word was spoken about the morrow. The pony man solemnly gave a toast: "To Billy, a fine quiet beast" and so to our spring mattresses.

Next morning our plight was discussed at length. Here we were, with supplies for three humans and one pony for five days, plus deer saddle, one farrier's kit, tent, cooking gear, etc., and no road, no house for miles. At that moment a sheep-dog came right into the tent, wagged his tail, gulped the breakfast remains, and departed, as a voice shouted something which sounded like, "Come in to heel!"

Outside stood a very tall lean man, and despite the time of day he was persuaded, without much difficulty, to come in and have some refreshment. The sad story of the garron was told and the reply: "Well, well, now. Well, well, he must have been lonely" (this with a quiet smile). MacPhee the shepherd, for such was his name, had walked over from Strathan to see his brother at Inverie (a matter of 24 miles), spent the night with him and was on his return journey. This he did once a year and it was indeed lucky for us that he had chosen that particular day. He said the pony would possibly be back at Strathan by this time and would be caught by the shepherds there; if not, he would pick him up on his way. This was a load off our minds, but how were we to transport all our gear now?

"Well," said MacPhee, "Mr Reddie, the factor at Inverie, is a very kind gentleman and you should go and ask his help." The shepherd then said he would have to be going, as he was not quite so young and it would be late before he arrived at Strathan, and off he started, as if on a 2-mile walk, over the track which had taken us two days!

The original plan to go to Barrisdale, Loch Hourn, and Loch Quoich was now out of the question, so it had to be Inverie. If we could borrow a pony to transport all our goods and chattels down to the pier, and if the mail boat did call on Wednesday, there would be little trouble in getting to Mallaig, whence it was only a two-hours train journey to Spean Bridge. Once there, we were only 29 miles from our cars at Strathan and could possibly hire transport. But would the unfaithful Billy be waiting for us? Perhaps it had been a good idea to insure the beast. Assuming all was well and Billy sound in wind and limb, the owner could be advised to collect him. If he was not at Strathan there would be nothing for it but to search that tremendous track of wild mountain country at the head of Loch Arkaig – a somewhat difficult task. This we discussed as we walked towards Inverie.

It is a delightful place on the shore of Loch Nevis. The estate is beautifully kept, is well wooded right down to the loch, and masses of rhododendrons are everywhere. The climate is almost sub-tropical; palms grow in the gardens, and fruit, vegetables, and flowers resemble those grown in the far south.

The shepherd was correct. Mr and Mrs Reddie were very kind to us three now rather disreputable looking tramps, with our sorry story. We had coffee, then the factor got his jeep out and took us up the hill, and in a very short time we were back in Inverie with all our gear, ready to embark on the next morning's boat.

During the night the wind blew up, the loch was rough, and the launch could not come into the pier, so we had a most exciting journey in a small rowing boat, somewhat overloaded with four men and all the luggage. The sail on this cold but sunny morning was a treat to be remembered. The hills, dominated by our old friend Sgor na Ciche, were at their best. Beautiful Inverie Bay, with its white houses and background of green trees, was soon lost to view. We took our last look up Loch Nevis and thought, "The world is full of strife and trouble, but here is peace, and the tide will always be coming in if it isn't going out!"

Then we were out in the Sound of Sleat, with Skye and the mighty Coolin straight in front of us, and so to Mallaig with its hundreds of greedy gulls and permanent aroma of fish.

The train left soon after our arrival and then there was that most beautiful train journey in Scotland to enjoy, right down to Loch Sheil.

By early afternoon we were back at Spean Bridge, standing on the platform surrounded by piles of luggage, on top of which was the saddle. As the train steamed out all the passengers seemed to be thinking, "Now what have they done with their horse?"

Mrs MacFadzean's son hired, we were told. So the lady was found and nearly died laughing when told about the garron. "Yes," she said, "it would be all right but expensive to hire to Strathan because of the bad road and the brake would be just be returning with the school children." Just then the phone rang. A half shaft on the vehicle had broken at Kinlochleven and the brake would not be back that night. We were advised to try the postmaster. He was very helpful, but had a meeting that night, so phoned a friend.

Unfortunately that gentleman had an appointment with the dentist. We were now absolutely stumped. Then the postmaster had a bright idea. There was a dance at Achnarry that night and dances always brought the shepherds down from Strathan. He could get to Achnarry and back in time for his meeting and the shepherds would take us home. We were most grateful.

That evening we were fixed up in a barn with lots of rats for company and, later on, cook was sent to find the dance hall and contact the shepherds. The band was strong and the hall easy but the shepherds difficult. Then after much searching the sound of Gaelic Singing was heard coming from an ambulance with large red crosses painted on it. The patients seemed very cheery and turned out to be the shepherds having a party. "Mr Dougal himself and without his pony," was the first remark. "Yes, Billy is a fine quiet pony and enjoying his holiday at Strathan."

They would be delighted to take us up the glen when the dance finished, which would be 2, 3, or perhaps 4 a.m. Our place of rest was pointed out and they promised to call. Sleep was difficult with the rats making much noise. We dozed and looked out every half-hour, but it was pouring rain and very dark. By 5 a.m. all cars had departed and we at last fell asleep.

Next morning, or rather that morning, there was nothing for it – since the shepherds had forgotten about us – but that banker and cook should walk the 14 miles to pick up their cars. The leader still had the sole of his shoe tied up with strings and reluctantly had to stay behind.

It was a beautiful morning but a hard road. Good time was made and 5 miles on there was a cheering sight: away in the distance, swaying, lurching, and bouncing came the ambulance – very decent

111

of them, thought both. With a screeching of brakes the vehicle came to a stop and out of the cabin popped a weather-beaten smiling face.

"Where were you last night, boys? We were looking everywhere for you and it is a great pity you were not there, because it's a long walk you will now be having, but a grand day for it. And here we are off to the sales at Fort William. Billy is waiting for you – yes, a fine quiet pony." And with that the engine roared and the machine bounced and bumped down the road. Sitting, or rather half standing in the back and holding on grimly, were three shepherds. Perhaps walking was preferable after all!

Nine miles farther on the school was reached and there was the schoolmaster with his three pupils, making a garden. "Grand day," said he; "come in and have a cup of tea." But we explained we were rather pushed for time. "Perhaps you will be stalking garrons to-day," came the reply and, as we went on our way, we thought how nice it would be to teach at Strathan.

Billy required no stalking. There he was in the sheep fank, munching the tender grass, and he expressed neither pleasure nor displeasure when we approached, but stood quietly while the banker tried to climb on his back to be photographed.

"Good-bye, Billy," we said; and at that moment he spied new pasture, turned his back, and trotted off.

"A fine quiet pony. Yes, to be sure, a fine quiet pony!"

Chapter Six

World War 1

How War came about between Great Britain and Germany

Written for the young by H E LEGGE

Dollar Magazine Vol. XIV No. 53 – March 1915

Why are we at war? How did it come about just at this particular time?

On 28th June 1914 there happened a fatal tragedy.

On 4th August 1914 war was declared between Great Britain and Germany.

Let me put before you, very simply, a sketch of the events of the five weeks and two days between 28th June and 4th August; for the immediate cause of this war was the contention between Austria and Servia.

"Servia is a small but very ancient kingdom in the Balkan Peninsula." The Servian people belong to the family of Slav nations, and the vast country of Russia is the predominant Power of the Slav race. So Russia is the great big brother of little Servia.

Turn now to Austria and the country of Bosnia.

Long ago, Bosnia was part of the Servian kingdom; then Turkey wrested it from Servia, and a few years ago (in 1908) Austria annexed it; therefore it is now part of Austria.

On 28th June the heir to the throne of Austria, the Archduke Francis Ferdinand, and his wife paid a visit to Sarajevo, the capital of Bosnia, and drove in state, amid crowds, along the streets. He went thither in order to review three army corps, ready for action, which Austria had assembled.

At Sarajevo, as the Archduke and Duchess were driving along, shots were fired at them; both were fatally wounded; both died almost directly. The assassin, a young man, was arrested.

Still, what had that terrible murder to do with Servia? Sarajevo is not in Servia, but in Bosnia.

The Austrian official press declared (before there had been time for investigation and proof) that Servia was to blame; that the murder at Sarajevo was the outcome of a plot organised by Servia.

The Austrian Government conducted a secret inquiry, and on 23rd July Austria sent an ultimatum to Servia which made certain extremely severe demands. Our Secretary for Foreign Affairs, Sir Edward Grey, declared that "the murder of the Archduke called for sympathy with Austria," and Russia also admitted that some of these ten demands were reasonable enough. But there were two features in the Austrian ultimatum which disquieted those who wished to keep Europe at peace. The first was the insistence on a time-limit which was much too short, only forty-eight hours; the second was the fact that Austria demanded complete submission to her dictates. "I have never seen," said Sir Edward Grey, "one state address to another independent state, a document of so formidable a character." However, Great Britain, Russia and France all advised Servia to submit as far as she could, to go to the furthest possible point in meeting the demands of Austria.

Before the time-limit was up, the Servian Government replied to Austria, and conceded the greater part of her demands; but there were certain points which touched her very existence as an independent state; she could not yield on them, for if she did, the Servians would no longer be a free people. She offered to accept, on them, the arbitration of the Hague Tribunal or of the Great Powers.

Austria refused to accept this reply, and declared war against Servia on 28th July, exactly one month after the murder of the Archduke.

Austria and Servia, then, are at war, and why in the world should any other nation go to war too?

There was one huge nation which could not see Servia attacked without resentment, its big brother, Russia, chief of the Slav races. Latterly, during the war in the Balkans, the Russian Foreign Minister "had made it clear to the Austrian Government that war with Russia must inevitably follow an Austrian attack on Servia." So Russia became involved.

What of Germany? Germany had supported the cause of Austria against Servia. She had done so notably on 24th July, the day after Austria had sent her ultimatum to Servia. Therefore war between Austria and Russia involved Germany as Austria's ally. But matters could not stop here, for Russia too had an ally, France, therefore France was drawn in.

Thus we see Germany and Austria knew from the beginning, knew when Austria threatened Servia, and Germany backed her up; they knew that Russia would come in; they knew that France would come in as Russia's ally; therefore they knew that they were stirring up a European war.

Here we see Austria, Germany, Servia, Russia, France – all involved – but not Great Britain.

WHAT WAS GREAT BRITAIN DOING?

The British Government, through Sir Edward Grey, whose efforts during the recent Balkan wars had won for him the title of the "Peacemaker of Europe," was working incessantly for peace.

Remember that it was on 23rd July that Austria sent her ultimatum to Servia. Already, on 20th July, Sir Edward Grey had pressed upon the German Ambassador the importance, "if the peace of Europe was to be preserved, of Austria keeping her demand within reasonable limits." On 22nd July the German Foreign Secretary answered that he "considered it inadvisable that the Austro-Hungarian Government should be approached by the German Government on the matter." That was tantamount to saying that Germany would make no effort to restrain Austria. And so, without protest from Germany, the Austrian ultimatum was sent to Servia the very next day.

On 23rd July Sir Edward Grey, on learning from the Austrian Ambassador the nature of the demands of the ultimatum, seriously urged objections against the insertion of a time-limit. Two days later, the German Ambassador at Vienna was asked to inform the Austrian Foreign Minister of Sir Edward's suggestion for an extension to the time-limit. But the German Foreign Secretary replied that the Austrian Minister was away, and "there would be delay and difficulty in getting time-limit extended," and he "admitted quite freely that the Austro-Hungarian Government wished to give the Servians a lesson, and that they meant to take military action."

On 24th July Sir Edward Grey, having seen the text of the ultimatum, proposed that four Powers, none of them involved with Servia, should work together to effect "mediating or moderating influence" in his own words, that "Germany, France, Italy, and Great Britain, who had not direct interests in Servia, should act together for the sake of peace simultaneously in Vienna and St Petersburg."

Russia expressed willingness to stand aside while the Powers conferred; France agreed, Italy agreed, and Sir Edward Grey, on 26th July, invited the Ambassadors of France, Italy, and Germany to a conference with himself, "for the purpose of discovering an issue which would prevent complications."

France accepted, Italy accepted, Germany refused.

On 27th July Sir Edward Grey saw the German ambassador. It is sad now to read his words in his account of this interview telegraphed on that same day to Berlin. He warned the German Ambassador that "other issues might be raised that would supersede the dispute between Austria and Servia, and would bring other Powers in, and the war would be the biggest ever known, but as long as Germany would work to keep the peace I would keep closely in touch."

On the following day, 28th July, Austria declared war on Servia.

Britain now tried to prevent the war from spreading to other nations.

On 29th July Sir Edward Grey appealed to the German Chancellor. His words were – "His Excellency may rely upon it that this country will continue, as heretofore, to strain every effort to secure peace, and to avert the calamity we all fear. If he can induce Austria to satisfy Russia, and to abstain from going so far as to come into collision with her, we shall all join in deep gratitude to his Excellency for having saved the peace of Europe."

Italy also appealed to Germany to the same effect.

On that same day, 29th July, the German Government made certain proposals to Great Britain. We shall speak of them presently.

On 30th July Sir Edward Grey declined these proposals. But though constrained in honour to decline them, he made yet another "most earnest" appeal to the German Chancellor, and he added – "If the peace of Europe can be preserved and the present crisis safely passed, my own endeavour will be to promote some arrangement to which Germany could be a party, by which she could be assured that no aggressive or hostile policy would be pursued against her or her Allies by France, Russia and ourselves, jointly or separately." Thus Sir Edward Grey did all in his power, as a member of the British Government, to assure Germany of peaceful and friendly intentions towards her. What more could he have said?

Yet on the next day, 31st July, he did still more. He made a further strong appeal to Germany for European peace, and he suggested that the four disinterested Powers (Germany, France, Italy, and Great Britain) should offer to Austria to "undertake to see that she obtained full satisfaction of her demands on Servia, provided that they did not impair Servian sovereignty and the integrity of Servian territory." He asked Germany to find out whether Austria would agree to this. Russia had already stated that she would be willing to accept some such arrangement. Everything depended on the action of Germany.

On that day she sent an ultimatum to Russia.

Before sunrise next morning – at half-past three o'clock in the early morning of 1st August – the King of Britain and his Ministers made a last attempt to prevent war. "The King telegraphed a personal message to the Tsar," a heartfelt appeal, proffering his good offices. The Tsar returned an answer on the same day, "I would gladly have accepted your proposals, had not the German Ambassador this afternoon presented a note to my Government, declaring war." The Tsar added, "In this solemn hour I wish to assure you once more that I have done all in my power to avert war." The truth of this assertion, and of that made by the Russian Foreign Minister, that "no suggestion held out to him had been refused," is verified by the "Diplomatic Correspondence" (the White Paper) published for all the world to see, wherein also can be read the consent of Russia to the British formula for basis of mediation. Far different is the case with Germany and Austria; they had given either doubtful answers or refusals.

These official documents reveal how strenuously and untiringly Britain, through her representatives, worked for peace, and showed, too, who it was who thwarted those efforts.

Now we come back to the proposals made by Germany to Britain on that momentous day, 29th July. On that day the British Ambassador at Berlin, Sir Edward Goschen, was sent for by the German Chancellor who had just returned from a visit to the Kaiser at Potsdam. The Chancellor revealed to Sir Edward Goschen that the German Government was contemplating war with France, and further, wished to send an army upon France through Belgium. He then tried to secure the neutrality of Britain, and her consent to these designs, by proposing a bargain with her.

First, Britain was to keep quiet and not to interfere, on the understanding that Germany "aimed at no territorial acquisitions at the expense of France." Sir Edward Goschen "questioned His

Excellency about the French colonies." The Chancellor would not give the same assurance in regard to them.

Second, Britain was to consent to Germany sending an army through Belgium into France. Through Belgium! To consent to bargain away her obligation to Belgium, solemnly entered into by the Treaty of 1839! Moreover, Germany herself had signed that Treaty, she, too, had vowed to respect the neutrality of Belgium. Now she meant to be false to that pledge, and asked us to be the same.

Thus Britain was asked to be disloyal to friendship in the case of France, and false to her plighted word in the case of Belgium. And mark this – what trust could she place in Germany's promise that "when the war was over, Belgian integrity would be respected, if she had not sided against Germany"? She made that promise to Britain at the very moment of proposing to break her signed promise to Belgium.

As regards France – we had made an Entente Cordiale, a friendly agreement, with her in 1904. Therefore, the northern coasts of France were left unprotected; France knew that we, a friendly Power, did not mean to attack them. If a German Fleet "came down the English Channel, and bombarded and battered the unprotected coasts of France, we could not honourably stand aside, and see this going on practically within sight of our eyes, with our arms folded." (Sir Edward Grey.)

This, then, was Sir Edward Grey's answer as to France, authorised by the Cabinet, given to Germany on 3rd August – "If the German Fleet comes into the Channel, or through the North Sea, to undertake hostile operations against French coasts or shipping, the British Fleet will give all the protection in its powers."

Now, as regards Belgium – innocent, inoffensive Belgium – a happy little country, with cities containing most beautiful old architecture and treasures of art, independent, trusting to the honour of Britain, France, Austria, Prussia, and Russia, who had all signed that Treaty guaranteeing her integrity. All had pledged themselves never to violate her neutrality, never to attack her, nor to send an armed force across her borders.

On 31st July Sir Edward Grey, in view of this solemn Treaty, asked both France and Germany whether they meant to respect the neutrality of Belgium.

France responded – "French Government are resolved to respect the neutrality of Belgium."

Germany gave no answer.

On 3rd August Germany addressed a note to Belgium, threatening to treat her as an enemy if she resisted the violation of her territory.

Belgium, heroic little Belgium, "refused this as a flagrant violation of the law of nations," and the King of the Belgians sent an appeal to King George – "Remembering the numerous proofs of your Majesty's friendship . . . and the friendly attitude of Britain in 1870 . . . I make a supreme appeal to the diplomatic intervention of your Majesty's Government to safeguard the integrity of Belgium."

That was the appeal of Belgium to Britain, stretching out wronged hands for help.

And Britain, how did Britain respond?

Britain kept her bond.

On 4th August the British Government addressed a note to Germany repeating the request of 31st July, as to whether she meant to respect Belgian neutrality, and asking for a satisfactory answer by midnight. Should Germany refuse, "His Majesty's Government feel bound to take all steps in their power to uphold the neutrality of Belgium, and the observance of a Treaty to which Germany is as much a party as ourselves."

How did Germany respond?

Germany broke her bond. A German army invaded Belgium.

Britain accordingly went to war.

We are fighting to uphold faithfulness to the pledged word; to abolish that hateful spirit of aggressive militarism; to "enthrone the idea of public right as the governing idea of European politics."

Germany has broken her word to Belgium, broken it in blood and fire, slaughter, broken bodies, broken hearts, burning towns, shattered homes, overwhelming innocent women and children with a tide of cruelty and terror.

We in Britain have seen some of those stricken Belgians, some of that host of refugees.

In our anguish for our own dead, may we still thank God that we took the side of honour.

We pray – "Guide us, through all this terror; we entreat Thee, into truth and love."

"Hasten on, ye Ages blest," said the Fates to their spindles. –
VIRGIL

About the Author

Edith Legge was the daughter of James Legge, who was a missionary in China, a translator of Chinese classics into English and the first Professor of Sinology at Oxford University. Edith attended Dollar Academy and wrote several articles and poems for the *Dollar Magazine*. While the Legge family were in Dollar they lived in the house which is now the Rectory for St James the Great Scottish Episcopal Church. Wang T'ao, who assisted James Legge with translations, spent a year in Dollar and made sketches and notes about his experiences. Copies of these may be seen in Dollar Museum.

"Wiring"

By An Officer at the Front

From the "Manchester Guardian"

Dollar Magazine Vol. XIV No. 54 – June 1915

In days of peace, like every other citizen, I have often "wired" but the verb has new significance now. No longer does it mean the compression into twelve words of a message that Aunt Jane has arrived safely, but that the key of her trunk has been left on the parlour mantelpiece.

"Wiring" as we understand the term at the front, is really a sport – almost the only one we are allowed. It is quite as interesting as golf, and not nearly so expensive. All one needs are a few rolls of barbed wire and some posts; and these are supplied free by the War Office. A dark night is also to be desired, but it is not always obtainable. After the war I should like to meet the man who first twisted barbs on wire. I shall have great pleasure in telling him what I think of his misdirected energy. Meantime I can only say that his invention has added a zest to life in the trenches.

The game is usually begun by the commanding officer remarking to the major that "We'd better have some more wire out in front". The major passed on this hint to one of his captains who in turn whispers gently but firmly to the subaltern of No. 15 Platoon that any quantity of wire and posts will be at his disposal by midnight.

At midnight, accordingly, word is passed along the line of sentries that a working party is going out in front of their sections and in a few minutes six muffled figures creep over the parapet of the trench. Half an hour is spent carrying forward the materials for the night's task – posts, large and small, a pick, and coils of wire slung on their sticks; lastly a heavy wooden mallet and some sandbags to deaden the sound of the blows. Silently, and as accurately as it can be done in the dark, the distances are paced out and the stakes laid down just where they are to be driven in. Then the ground is broken at each place with the pick, and the real fun begins – hammering in the posts. In spite of sandbags and every other precaution, a certain amount of noise is unavoidable. All at once the night has become dreadfully still; even the distant rifle-fire has died down; and, of course, the moon comes out from behind the clouds. Poor old moon, how we abuse you at these times!

Dump! Dump! Dump! Slowly the post sinks into the ground. Dump! Dump! Dump! Till the officer says "That one'll do"; so the work goes on. All the while we have two men listening and watching a few yards away. One post after another is fixed, and still the enemy shows no sign of having heard us. Then "Phizz!" a star rocket rises from their trenches, lighting up all the ground between them and us. Promptly we drop flat, and are thankful for our dark background. "Phizz!" another rocket bursts, and lands quite near us. Then a machine-gun starts "pa-pa-pa-pa-pap." But evidently we haven't been spotted, for the five rounds are far wide of us. For a few minutes we lie quite still; then, as nothing more happens, we go on with the wiring, leaving the completion of the post-driving till the next night.

Now, the one and only good point about the actual wiring operations is its comparative noiselessness. If anyone doubts me, let him try to draw a yard of barbed wire off the first roll he sees at his ironmonger's, and then picture what the job is like when carried out in the dark. Either the barbs stick together, or three rounds of wire spring off the coil simultaneously and wind themselves round one's body like a boa-constrictor. Yet strange as it may appear, there is a certain amount of pleasure in "wiring". The prevailing feeling seems to be, "This should give the Allemande something to think about." Hands are cut and clothes are torn, but nobody seems to mind.

A good night's work done, we creep back to our trench, and send along the message, "working party in." Just before we drop behind the parapet we listen for a moment. Faintly across the fields from the enemy's trenches comes a sound we recognise: Dump! Dump! Dump! The beggars are at the same game as ourselves!

Extract from Letter from the Front

By Edward Radford (F.P.),
A. and S. Highlanders

Dollar Magazine Vol. XIV No. 54 – June 1915

"Thursday 6th May 1915

" . . . This is the twelfth day in the trenches, and twice we have been in action. But the shelling has been about as bad as the fighting. The German artillery is very strong, and their gas bombs quite an ingenious patent, but we have a remedy for it. That's about all I can tell you of our doings, but I can tell you my feelings as regards what we have gone through. It has brought me closer to God than ever I was before; how little our lives seemed to count. He held them in the hollow of His hand, and at His will certain ones dropped, perhaps never to rise again, whilst others were shattered by shells. The first action was bigger than the second, the Germans were expecting us, and the bullets literally rained past us. It must have been God's will that more of us were not killed. The papers will only call it a slight skirmish, but our ranks were badly thinned.

"But it was whilst the big shells and shrapnel burst round the trenches playing havoc with them, and we were sitting still with nothing to do but think and wonder when the next one would drop, that my feelings and thoughts were as already described. I forgot to mention we also repulsed an attack, but we gave the Germans no chance and altogether it was a miserable attempt on their part. Our blood was up on account of our previous heavy shelling, and other things, and we were only too eager to get a chance of paying them out."

Fed Up

By W. K. H.

Dollar Magazine Vol. XVI No. 64 December 1917

Dexter, the erstwhile faithful Gunner Dexter, has grossly deceived me. After months – I could very soon have said years – of devoted service, ministering to my every want, anticipating my most unreasonable whim, sharing all my unavoidable perils, he has at last let me down. It happened like this. From the *dolce far niente* of the battery position they sent me to spend a few weeks amidst the perils and excitements of the Waggon Line, while the Captain changed places with me and went to be fattened by the mess cook at the guns.

"Your servant, Dexter, can cook for you down there, I suppose?" said the Major, and in my foolish innocence I replied "I'm sure he'll be able to do all I need, sir. It will do me good to live on bully and biscuits for a time." Dexter, on being interrogated, signified rather sheepishly that if I wouldn't be hypercritical he thought he might manage.

One wild, tempestuous afternoon I leapt (with my groom's assistance) to the saddle and splashed the few miles to the Waggon Line, while Dexter with my other necessaries followed in the mess cart. My billet I found on the bedraggled fringe of a large town. The "dining-room" opened direct upon a miry road by which endless strings of supply lorries and G.S. wagons bump and grind and jingle about their business. Its door and antique windows of reinforced cardboard peered straight into the eye of the prevailing wind, and it seemed I was to be joint tenant with a young but lusty cyclone. On some of the bright spring days that followed, the steam from my tea cup whirled to leeward like the smoke from a destroyer's funnels, till I shook off my torpor and stuffed up some of the crannies with summer clothing.

Simpleton that I was, I dared the elements again on a trip to the neighbouring canteen and purchased a tin of condensed milk, a box of Bath Olivers, and a soup square, stifling the reproaches of my Spartan conscience by assuring it that this outlay was justifiable when my house-warming was in view.

When Dexter arrived, I told him that I should like "something to eat" (those were my very words) about eight o'clock. Then I went out to look at my horses . . . Looking at horses always exhausts me, particularly if I have to do it under the sardonic eye of a taciturn and capable Sergeant-Major, and I returned to my new home, Boreas Lodge, eagerly anticipating a slice of bully beef and a Bath Oliver in the lee of the cold black stove. At eight o'clock I sat down with a waving candle at my elbow, and Dexter brought in a plate of soup.

"Hullo!" said I, dismayed a little, for I was trying to live on the pay of a subaltern, "you have already used the soup square?" "Yessir," said Dexter. The soup was excellent; it radiated a pleasant internal warmth that seemed to temper the bitterness of the wind that beat upon the surface of my person.

"D'you like fried onions, sir?" asked Dexter, as he whipped away my plate. Now, from childhood I have longed to eat fried onions in large quantities, but have denied myself this pleasure, from cowardice or consideration. The solitude of the Waggon Line seemed to afford the opportunity of a life-time; and I said I did. Two minutes later, after mysterious clatterings in the kitchen, Dexter appeared with an astounding plateful – meat of some unrecognisable variety, such as the poet sings was never yet on land or sea; costly exotic vegetables, the potato, the sprout, the Heinz bean, not to mention the Spanish onion in luscious pungent shavings; smoking islands around which flowed a rich and precious tide of sauces, condiments long since deemed mythical, surviving in name alone in canteen lists and other works of fancy. And from this mounded platter there drifted and tossed to leeward a stream of vapour heavy with savours as the zephyrs of Cockayne. A sweet followed - a nameless lure, an anonymous temptation . . . . As I realised with a start that I had finished it, I determined to reprimand Dexter with the utmost severity, and hailed him in my battery gun-drill tones.

"Yessir," he answered, and dived in with a savoury – not one of your active service savouries, a glutinous, lukewarm splash of melted ration cheese clasping a wedge of damp toast; but a creation in which cheese was represented but as a reminiscence, chastened, etherealised. And then, indignant as I was, Dexter taunted me with a Bath Oliver and butter, and put the flourish to his impertinence with a cup of such coffee as our dreams are made of . . . . So it goes on, day after day. The people at the guns pity me; they send down pencilled notes saying they hope I am all right, and cheerio, and so forth. Dexter professes a childish diffidence about each forthcoming meal; I meet him returning from Q.M.S. stores with our rations – his and mine – in their natural state in a sandbag over his shoulder; and he never fails to tell me how poor they are. I have discoursed to him of plain living and high thinking, and his comment is ever "Very good, sir," before he returns to the kitchen to conspire anew against my figure. . . . I am ashamed to accompany waggon loads of ammunition up to the guns; my favourite charger looks at me askance, and grunts as I clamber to the saddle. I ought to return there rather lean and tired – too bright-eyed, and a little gaunt, you know – proving the wear and tear of life at the Waggon Line, but Dexter has let me down.

132

His defence is, I daresay, that he is trying experiments upon me – his bloke; but what excuse is that for me, who show only too plainly that they are all successful?

About the Author

W.K.H. These are the initials of William Kersley Holmes. A Former Pupil of Dollar Academy and responsible for the words of the School Song 'Here in a Fair Green Valley', WKH worked in banking and later publishing. He was a prolific poet and writer of books and articles about his beloved Scottish hills. 'Ballads of Field and Billet' appeared while he was serving as a gunner during WW1. His classic 'Tramping Scottish Hills' is still much read. The Holmes family lived at one time in the house beside Brian Devlin's butcher shop and were famed locally for having pet owls which flew freely about inside the house.